RADICAL
FORGIVENESS

RADICAL FORGIVENESS

Antoinette Bosco

ORBIS BOOKS
Maryknoll, New York 10545

Founded in 1970, Orbis Books endeavors to publish works that enlighten the mind, nourish the spirit, and challenge the conscience. The publishing arm of the Maryknoll Fathers & Brothers, Orbis seeks to explore the global dimensions of the Christian faith and mission, to invite dialogue with diverse cultures and religious traditions, and to serve the cause of reconciliation and peace. The books published reflect the views of their authors and do not represent the official position of the Maryknoll Society. To learn more about Maryknoll and Orbis Books, please visit our website at www.maryknollsociety.org.

Published in 2009 by Orbis Books, Maryknoll, New York 10545-0308.

Manufactured in the United States of America.

Library of Congress Cataloging-in-Publication Data

Bosco, Antoinette, 1928-
    Radical forgiveness / Antoinette Bosco.
    p. cm.
        ISBN 978-1-57075-815-7 (pbk.)
        1. Forgiveness of sin. 2. Forgiveness—Religious
    aspects—Christianity. I. Title.
        BT795.B67 2009
  234'.5—dc22
                                                2008034415

*With humility and gratitude I dedicate this book to
family, teachers, and friends
who gave me the many soul-gifts I needed
to believe in forgiveness when life challenged me,
and I give a special thank you to my many spirit-friends,
like Charles Grosso, Kevin Cronin, Vonda White,
and my editor Michael Leach.*

CONTENTS

INTRODUCTION

This is a book I didn't expect to write. For one reason, I rather felt I had already written much on the subject of forgiveness from a very personal perspective. My life had put me on a fire of personal pain, trying to recover from the tragic deaths of two sons—one by suicide, and the other, with his wife, murdered. I had struggled long and hard with how to survive such unbelievable torment. Because from an early age I had relied on the teachings of my Lord Jesus to help me get through difficult times, now too I felt his help, leading me to believe that I was not alone. Even more, through the decades I kept learning that I could trust him to help me see where I needed to go. Now again I believed he was helping me take the actions that would bring healing, and each step was clearly marked with directions—Forgive! Forgive your troubled Peter, forgive the young killer of your John and Nancy, forgive yourself.

Because I was a writer, I started to put some of my questions down on paper. How I was to learn to forgive when I had no definition for forgiveness that really worked for something as horrific as this? All I had known in the past about forgiveness struck me as being quite naïve and actually arrogant. All well and good to say "I forgive" when what you are forgiving has not caused devastating and seemingly permanent harm. But what about when the injury has ripped your very soul apart?

And yet, I knew I would be lost if I stayed in the dark, unmoving, stuck world that traps the unforgiving. I began to write, pouring out my pain on pages of paper, hoping, I suppose, that transferring the torments to print would in some way help me let go of them. I showed a little of what I was writing to Neil Klupfel, the founder of Twenty-Third Publications. He told me to continue the writing and send it to him. I did, and it became a book entitled *The Pummeled Heart: Finding Peace through Pain.* To my surprise, my all my meditations and prayers, solidified in print, marked the beginning of a true healing process. I felt the Lord had truly come to rescue me and I became restored enough to believe I could now try to get good out of my pain by trying to help others who had also had to deal with unbelievable tragedies in their lives.

At the same time, I was learning something else. There is no past tense to forgiveness. I cannot say I "forgave" the killer of my children and then be done with it, because I really don't know where I will stand tomorrow. The same is true for all of us. Each day has to be a renewal of our decision to forgive, because we face the jagged edges of our world every single day. We know not the day or the hour when soul-deep pain can strike again—from evil coming from any source—demolishing all belief that forgiveness makes sense or is justified.

I meditated on how the convert-writer G. K. Chesterton spoke of radical forgiveness, especially on how he connected Christianity to both crime and forgiveness.

> A sensible pagan would say that there were some people one could forgive, and some one couldn't; a slave who stole wine could be laughed at; a slave who betrayed his benefactor could be killed, and cursed even after he was killed. In so far as the act was pardonable, the man was pardonable. That again is rational and even refreshing; but it is a dilution ...Christianity came in here startlingly, and divided the crime from the criminal. The criminal we must forgive unto seventy times seven. The crime we must not forgive at all...The more I considered Christianity, the more I found that while it had established a rule and order, the chief aim of that order was to give room for good things to run wild.

"Good things to run wild!" I believe *that* is the fruit of radical forgiveness, the fact that such forgiveness makes it possible for "good things" to come back into our lives; and then, when we hand our forgiveness to Christ, he can "run wild with it," even opening heaven, as he did for the good thief.

Why did Luke include in his gospel this amazing happening on Calvary? I believe it was because this is more than just the story of two thieves. It may even be the most profound story we find in the passion event, a story that has to do with nothing less than the salvation of humanity, with who loses heaven and who wins it. Consider where Luke places Jesus—in the center, between two sinners. These men are not just thieves, but representatives of the entire human race.

On one side is the person entrenched in his own self, letting all the human sins he has chosen to live by be not simply exposed but also justified by his self-righteous holding onto them.

But on the other side of Jesus is the person who acknowledges his sins because he now finds himself confronted by utter goodness. In the face of this, his hardness disappears and, seeing how different his life could—and should—have been, he makes a choice. He accepts responsibility for his crimes and, turning to the One he knows to be innocent, the One he recognizes as having a "kingdom" in paradise, he in effect seeks forgiveness by asking to be remembered when Jesus comes into his kingdom.

Jesus, who would have every human ever created be forever in his kingdom, doesn't respond with, "First, you have to be punished." No, he "runs wild" with this, and says to the repentant sinner words that have resounded down through the centuries: *"This day*—you will be with me in paradise!"

Paradise begins the moment we realize forgiveness.

This scene in Luke's gospel is profoundly touching, for it shows the power of forgiveness and highlights its two essential aspects: one must ask, One then gives.

Also memorable is the sadness in the silence from the other side, the unforgiving thief, permanently lost.

Here we have the mystery of forgiveness laid out, placed in the center of the universe: between a rejection and a plea—an embrace. It is clearly the most important message Christ came to earth to give us—that there is no entering into his Father's kingdom if one remains hardened and unforgiving. When Jesus told Peter he had to forgive seventy times seven times, it wasn't a numbers game. Jesus was teaching that forgiveness is as intrinsic to life as our breathing. Forgiveness has to be a continuous way of life. Forgiveness has to be always in the present tense, for it is never done.

Few people, thank God, have to deal with forgiving someone who has murdered a loved one, or a beloved child who is defeated in life and ends his or her pain by committing suicide. But all of us must deal on a regular basis with thoughts about people we feel have hurt us, abandoned us, spoken badly about us, hurt our feelings, damaged our reputations, manipulated, provoked, or just plain annoyed us. They can be parents, relatives, friends, bosses, employees, even strangers.

But it is not these people we need to forgive so much as our thoughts about them, the angry, unforgiving thoughts that gnaw at our consciousness, burn us, haunt us, won't let us go, because we can't let *them* go. I have learned that radical forgiveness, asked for and given, seventy times seven times, is the only way out of that prison.

If you hold resentment, large or small, toward anyone, this book is for you.

Antoinette Bosco
Brookfield, Connecticut

1
JESUS' MISSION—
TO REVEAL HIS FATHER

The object of Jesus was to induce men to base all life on God ...that we should think life out, that we should come face to face with God and see him for what he is...He means us to go about things in God's way—forgiving our enemies, cherishing kind thoughts about those who hate us or despise us or use us badly, praying for them.

—T. R. Glover

During his public ministry, Jesus clearly shook things up with his teachings about God, whom he called "Abba," a term that could be translated as "Dad." Jesus' words and actions especially challenged the religious teachers and leaders of his times and homeland. As the late Professor John Macquarrie said in one of the religion classes I attended at Oxford University, "the traditional way of talking about God, in terms of power and rule, needed to be rethought." And that's what Jesus was doing. "He brought a massive correction to the concept of God."

Imagine how radical Jesus' words were. He spoke of God as our loving Father, not a punishing policeman, but the divine parent who wanted his children to be just like him. And he gave them the "formula," so to speak, for how this could happen. They had to be generous, fair, kind, merciful, forgiving, and peacemakers.

But, even more, to ensure they were like their loving Father, they had to love their enemies, do good to those who hated them and pray for those who persecuted and insulted them. Henri-Daniel Rops, in his 1954 book *Jesus and His Times*, expressed how radical a teaching this was:

> This love is a complete reversal of our human tendencies, for it is not the love which we bear to our family and friends; it is not even the love which a generous heart feels for the unhappy and the sinful. Nor does its reference to pardoning offences mean that kind of forgiveness which time and forgetfulness bring us. It means a superhuman turning inside out, a humiliation of our nature and of our legitimate pride, the kissing of the hand which strikes us.

As we know from the gospels, Jesus' strange, new message wasn't very popular with most people. In fact, it got him executed. "Old gods linger on," as Professor Macquarrie put it.

From a very young age, I used to think a lot about the treatment Jesus got during his life on earth that led him to be executed brutally on the cross. Sometimes I would wonder why God would do this to someone he very specially called his *Son*. Then, in my young adult years, I read a marvelous book called *The Everlasting Man* by the British writer G. K. Chesterton. The book so influenced me that I underlined sections from beginning to end. In discussing the coming of Jesus and the drama that unfolded with his teachings and ultimate walk to the cross, Chesterton wrote: "Since that day it has never been quite enough to say that God is in his heaven and all is right with the world; since the rumor that God had left his heavens to set it right."

Chesterton's point was that if all was right with the world, God would not have had to send his Son to show us *how* to make the world right. That's what Jesus was about, and what an assignment it was! Take forgiveness, for example. The Son, bringing the message of the Father to the people, underscored forgiveness, making it quite clear that this was not a negotiable order. Jesus must have known that this was one of the critical commandments, since it is human nature to want to "even the score" in the case of crime or abuse or anything else that makes a person feel "victimized." He probably knew, too, that forgiveness was one of his teachings that would be seen as outrageously infringing upon God's territory, and his punishment for that would be severe, stopping at nothing short of the death penalty.

After my son Peter died, I was constantly praying to the Lord to help me forgive him for killing himself. I was in such severe pain, and I screamed at God, too, asking him why he had let such torment be my youngest son's fate. I realized I was facing a new life that would include a new relationship with God, for better or worse, but I didn't know who I was going to become. All that I knew was that I would never again be the person I had been. I was seized with a kind of compulsion to learn ever more about Jesus Christ, and especially what he had meant by forgiveness now that my old definition had come to seem something of a fairy tale.

How God Is Listening to Us

Unexpectedly, I saw an ad in a Catholic paper about a summer Religious Studies program at Oxford University in England. I still can hardly believe my response. I put the paper down, picked up the phone, got some more information about the courses and professors, and said, "Sign me up." Then I took a temporary leave from my job as editor of a secular newspaper in Connecticut and began packing for England. This was in 1992. I had no way of knowing then that I would eventually come to see this sudden decision of mine as no "accident." I found so much healing and peace in the company of the faculty and my fellow "students," most of whom were professors in some area of religious work.

One professor who became a permanent friend was the world-respected New Testament scholar, Dr. N. T. Wright, as he identifies himself (Nicholas Thomas, for the curious). He was addressing the question of what kind of authority the New Testament possesses. In a personal conversation I had with him, he spoke of how the research ahead of him would involve tackling the New Testament questions that still need greater study. The biggest question, of course, has to do with Jesus. That remains as significant an issue now as it ever was. What were Jesus' actual aims? Not enough attention has been given to what he was trying to accomplish.

Why did Jesus die? What were the agendas that put him on the cross?

Jesus died a criminal's death. "So," I asked Dr. Wright, "how do you explain the early Christians?" His answer was that you can't without the resurrection. Something happened on Easter morning. And whatever happened radically changed the world. The early church spread like wildfire. Was this just a chance occurrence, a historical fluke? No. They, the first Christians, aimed for this. They were trying to tell people in all corners of society about the *God* revealed in Jesus. They were a group of people grasped by the belief that the hope of Israel had come true because they saw in Jesus the new Moses who had produced the new exodus, redeeming his people from being slaves of the real enemy, Satan.

Dr. Wright also spoke to me of the so-called "hidden years" of Jesus, the mystery of what he was doing from age twelve to about age thirty, since nothing is contained in the New Testament about this period of Jesus' life. "They remain the silent years," Dr. Wright noted. "But whatever else Jesus was doing in that period, he got to know the Old Testament like the back of his hand... taking many teachings of the Old Testament but giving them a bit of a new twist authoritatively to affirm his message.

"I think there is good reason to think Jesus did know he was the Messiah," added Dr. Wright. "His message was an invitation to choose a new world view, a new way of being human."

I found all of this intriguing. It made me want to go back to the gospels and to the writings of Jesus scholars to rediscover this man who called God his Father, and even more intimately, his "Dad."

Shortly after this conversation with Dr. Wright, at a used book sale on a street near Oxford, I picked up and bought a book by a theologian named T. R. Glover, titled *The Jesus of History*, and published in 1917. The author's words, written so long ago, especially underscored for me who Jesus was and what he was saying about his—and our—relationship with God, the Father:

> The object of Jesus was to induce men to base all life on God…Jesus urges—that we should think life out, that we should come face to face with God and see him for what he is and accept him. He means us to live a life utterly and absolutely based on God—life on God's lines of peacemaking and ministry, the "denial of self," a complete forgetfulness of self in surrender to God, obedience to God, faith in God, and the acceptance of the sunshine of God's Fatherhood. He means us to go about things in God's way—forgiving our enemies, cherishing kind thoughts about those who hate us or despise us or use us badly, praying for them.
>
> This takes us right back into the common world, where we have to live in any case; and it is there he means us to live with God—not in trance, but at work, in the family, in business, shop and street, doing all the little things and all the great things that God wants us to do, and glad to do them just because we are his children and he is our Father. Above all, he would have us "think like God"; and to reach this habit of "thinking like God," we have to live in the atmosphere of Jesus, "with him."

There it was again, the rule of our Father God, which mandated "forgiving our enemies." And of course, I could accept that, because my son Peter had not been my enemy. My problem with forgiveness was not linked to my "enemy," but to my loved one. At that point, I didn't have any "enemies" that I knew of, though I sometimes wondered if I weren't becoming my own enemy. I could relate all too well to the words of C. S. Lewis, written after his beloved wife Joy died: "For in grief, nothing stays 'put.' One keeps on emerging from a phase, but it always recurs. Round and round. Everything repeats. Am I going in circles, or dare I hope I'm on a spiral?"

At Oxford, I was fortunate enough to discover yet another friend who was deeply empathetic and understanding of my pain and struggle to forgive my son Peter. He was one of our teachers, the Right Rev. Richard Holloway, bishop of Edinburgh, who, on hearing my story, acknowledged to me how difficult life can be, saying, "The universe didn't come with an explanatory leaflet attached. Christ is encountered, never explained."

In talking to me of Peter's suicide, Bishop Holloway didn't emphasize forgiveness, but he said something that put me on the road to finding it. He pointed out that after we acknowledge the loss we experience and the wounding that takes place when a loved one dies, we must "gather together the life to affirm and conclude it. We must be celebrants of their lives," and they will from that time on always be remembered. Then anger and unforgiveness will end, for in celebration there is no room for such "God-defying" conditions.

I returned home, back to my family and to my editorial position, after what had been a healing, life-altering experience at Oxford. Truly, the need to "forgive" my son Peter was done with. He would always be in my heart, thoughts, and prayers, enfolded in love and a sense of celebration and gratitude for the years he was with us on earth. Period. But then came the phone call from Montana just one year later—the sheriff telling me that my son John and his wife Nancy had been murdered, shot to death in the middle of the night by someone using a 9-millimeter semi-automatic gun in their home as they slept. There are no words to describe the horror of hearing these words. No doubt it can go without saying, though, that the last thing on my mind then and in the weeks that followed was forgiveness.

We were to find out four months later that this apparently random act of cold-blooded murder was in fact not so random, but was actually a crime carried out by Joseph "Shadow" Clark, the eighteen-year-old son of the people from whom my kids had purchased the house a few months earlier. During those months, my then five living children and I had struggled with the terrible question of how we would respond if the killer were ever caught. Now the day had come, and we realized that, without question, the young man would be facing the death penalty.

In our grief, we knew we would struggle forever with "forgiveness." But we also knew we did not believe in killing, not as Shadow Clark had done, nor as the state would do to him. We all agreed that we would send a letter to the judge, telling him that we did not want this young man killed. We left it to my daughter Mary to write it, and she expressed our feelings very clearly:

In the ten months that have passed since the horrifying, devastating events of August 12, 1993, we have all struggled, despite our complete heartache and aching grief, not to sink into any desire for vengeance. We made the decision early on that Shadow Clark would not destroy any more of our family by dragging us down into bloodthirsty hatred. Our focus is on healing. We feel terrible sadness when we think of how Shadow Clark, such a young man, has destroyed his own life along with the lives of others. This is very difficult, *but we hope one day to understand what forgiveness in a case like this might mean* ...

The Difficult Journey in Confronting Forgiveness

As the new year of 1994 began, this is where I was, struggling to get a new handle on forgiveness. I wanted desperately to better understand why speaking of forgiveness was so important to Jesus, especially since it was clear from the gospels that forgiveness, as part of the way we treat others, has a lot to do with how God will treat us. Our way of living has to be such that we are, in effect, asking God for forgiveness. As we read in St. Matthew's gospel, Jesus says we must feed the hungry, care for the sick, visit those in prison, and so forth, and if we defiantly say no, here is his answer:

> "Truly I tell you, just as you did not do it to one of the least of these, you did not do it to me." And these will go away into eternal punishment, but the righteous into eternal life.

And consider Matthew's account of Jesus' parable of the servant who, having been forgiven by his master for his debt, refuses to forgive the debtor who owes him. When the master hears of this, he asks, "Should you not have had mercy on your fellow slave, as I had mercy on you?" Then the master turns the unforgiving servant over to be tortured. Jesus concludes the parable by stating, "So my heavenly Father will also do to every one of you, if you do not forgive your brother or sister from your heart."

I had so often heard those words, and thought I understood them, but now I saw in a new way how complex forgiveness is. We have to *earn* God's forgiveness, and we do that by forgiving our brothers and sisters, but we can't unless we believe in forgiveness, and that's where Jesus comes in. This means that we'll never "get" what Jesus was saying unless we seek to understand who he was. Dr. Wright at Oxford had alluded to this when he said he was researching and writing a new book about Jesus, "who towers over history and calls people to follow him in changing the world." He had said his book would be titled *Jesus and the Victory of God*, because Israel's history had reached its "great climatic moment" with the work of Jesus. I hoped I wouldn't have to wait too long for that book.

Finding True Understanding of Forgiveness in the Holy Land

Then, unexpectedly, I got a phone call from an acquaintance, a lovely woman I had met at a writer's conference. She told me to "get ready to go to Israel."

As she explained, there was to be a very high-level conference for Christians and Jews in Jerusalem, a first-time-ever such gathering. She worked for the Ministry of Tourism in Israel, and they wanted to have Christian writers attending the meeting, which was focusing on how social and scientific issues in an ever more secularized society are challenging religious leadership. She said speakers would include important officials from the Vatican, and added that, by the way, if I accepted this free trip, I could also arrange to take part in a tour of the Holy Land.

It was clearly one of those offers one couldn't refuse! To my surprise, the top official from the Vatican was Joseph Cardinal Ratzinger, now our Pope Benedict XVI, and his opening words were, for me, startling:

> The history of the relationship between Israel and Christendom is drenched with blood and tears. It is a history of mistrust and hostility, but also—thank God—a history marked again and again by attempts at forgiveness, understanding, and mutual acceptance. After Auschwitz, the message of reconciliation and acceptance permits no deferral. Even if we know that Auschwitz is the gruesome expression of an ideology that not only wanted to destroy Judaism but also hated and sought to eradicate from Christianity its Jewish heritage, the question remains: What could be the reason for so much historical hostility between those who actually must belong together because of their faith in the one God and commitment to his will?

Cardinal Ratzinger continued by stating:

> We stand here before a paradox. The faith of Israel was directed to universality. Since it is devoted to

the one God of all men, it also bore within itself the promise to become the faith of all nations. But the law, in which it was expressed, was particular, quite concretely directed to Israel and its history; it could not be universalized in this form...Jesus opened up the law quite theologically conscious of, and claiming to be, acting as Son, with the authority of God himself, in innermost unity with God the Father...Jesus' interpretation of the law makes sense only if it is interpretation *with divine authority* ...The quarrel between Jesus and the Jewish authorities of his time is finally not a matter of this or that particular infringement of the law, but rather of Jesus' claim to act *auctoritate divina*, indeed, to be this *auctoritas* himself. "I and the Father are one."

Cardinal Ratzinger went on to note that "only when one penetrates to this point can he also see the tragic depth of the conflict" that has unfortunately too often prevailed in Christian-Jewish relations.

Then this cardinal, who had been a youngster when the Nazis took over his land of Germany and who is now our pope, spoke personally of forgiveness: "Already as a child...I could not understand how some people wanted to derive a condemnation of the Jews from the death of Jesus because the following thought had penetrated my soul as something profoundly consoling: Jesus' blood raises no calls for retaliation, but calls all to reconciliation"— which is where the forgiveness Jesus speaks of comes in.

On that stage in an amphitheater in Jerusalem Cardinal Ratzinger concluded, to thundering applause: "Jews and Christians should accept each other in profound inner reconciliation, neither in disregard of their faith nor in its denial, but out of the depth of faith itself. In their mutual reconciliation they should become a force for peace in and for the world."

Because I was present as a specially invited reporter, I had been given a seat in the front row. When the cardinal from the Vatican ended his talk, I, along with several others, was able to get to the stage immediately, where, with a gracious smile, he clasped our hands in turn warmly. I was also able to get a copy of his talk, which I considered an honor. Before leaving Israel, I was privileged to walk where Jesus had walked in his lifetime, to see where he had been crucified and where he had been buried. I was on my way to accepting forgiveness, as Jesus told us to forgive, and could bring that "healing" back home with me.

Soon after I returned home, I discovered that my Oxford professor, N. T. Wright, had now published his book *Jesus and the Victory of God*. I read it and found it to be the perfect "next step" for me in what I had come to call my "forgiveness journey." Dr. Wright wrote about the parable of the prodigal son, saying that it was about "exile and restoration," which was the central drama that "Israel believed herself to be acting out." The story of the prodigal son says that this hope

> is now being fulfilled, but it does not look like what was expected . . . Israel's history is turning its long-awaited corner . . . the true Israel is coming to its senses and returning to its Father . . . this is happening within the ministry of Jesus himself; and those who oppose it are the enemies of the true people of God . . .

In other words, it is time for the Gentiles to come in, because Israel's exile is at last over, and she has been restored...God is bringing the destiny of Israel to completion in the person of Jesus.

With the end of exile comes forgiveness, because "exile was the punishment for sin...return from exile means Israel's sins have been forgiven." After quoting both Jeremiah and Ezekiel to back up this insight, Dr. Wright goes on to say:

What Jesus was offering...was a new world order, the end of Israel's long desolation, the true and final "forgiveness of sins," the inauguration of the kingdom of God...and if Israel is really to imitate her heavenly Father, she must learn to love people and pray for them...Forgiveness was to be the central character of the life of those loyal to Jesus.

Now comes the real problem with what Jesus was saying. "Love and mercy, as practical codes of living, are to characterize Israel as the true people of the creator. People like that are the ones he will vindicate when he comes into his kingdom. Forgiveness is to be the hallmark of all social relationships," explains Dr. Wright, emphasizing that for "that claim to be made good, Jesus' people would have to enact this forgiveness among themselves." Then he adds, as an aside, "One only has to live a short time in a society where forgiveness is not even valued in theory—where, for instance, 'losing face' is regarded as one of the greatest misfortunes—to realize how revolutionary this challenge really is."

The Son of God "pitched his tent, as John puts it, in our midst," Dr. Wright maintains, because "the creator, according to some of the most ancient Jewish beliefs, grieved so much over creation gone wrong, over humankind in rebellion, over thorns and thistles and dust and death, that he planned from the beginning the way by which he would rescue his world, his creation, his history, from its tragic corruption and decay..." He sent his Son Jesus, whose life, death, and resurrection was the "beginning of the new creation...bursting in on the old."

As Christians we believe that God disclosed himself in Christ. In the words of Norman Goodall, a British World War I veteran, recognized in the last century as an outstanding missionary statesman, "It is in Jesus that there is life in the midst of death, Eternal Life entering into time, the Life which is of the very essence of God manifesting itself amidst our mortality. In Jesus, I come as near to seeing the Face of God as mortal man can ever do in this world."

Jesus himself made clear who he was—"I and the Father are One." And he carried out his mission—to introduce his Father again to this world.

The Sermon on the Mount moves from Divine possibility to human enactment... With God's blessing, common people do their best to redeem an imperfect world. It is not something we wait for, but something we create.

—Erik Kolbell

2
THE CRUCIAL FACE-OFF—
EVIL VS. FORGIVENESS

Worse is he who, when reviled, reviles again.
Who, when reviled, does not revile again,
  a two-fold victory wins.
He seeks the good both of the other and himself.
                                    —*Buddha*

I f ever there were a challenging question that we humans faced, it would have to be why God, whom we call "Father," permits evil to exist powerfully and go on continually in the midst of his divine creation. A father is supposed to be good, caring, and loving of his children. So, when we say "father," and mean our Father God, shouldn't we expect him to be infinitely good? And doesn't that give us a right to expect that he would not permit evil to take root and flourish in his world, bringing pain, torment, chaos, destruction, and every negative possibility imaginable to his people? Is it possible to forgive God for the evil and torment that flourishes in his creation?

After the devastating New York World Trade Center attack in 2001, which killed nearly three thousand people, it became almost a mantra for President George Bush to say that we would defeat "the evil ones." This was a scary choice of words. It was a constant reminder that any one of us, at any time, could be the victim of evil. No wonder a relative of one of the victims—and many others—asked: "Where was God when the planes were flying? Couldn't an all-powerful God have stopped them, so that all those innocent people would not have had to die?"

I asked that same question when I got the news of the murders of my son John and his wife Nancy. Couldn't God have stopped the bullets coming from a 9-millimeter semiautomatic gun in the hands of an eighteen-year old before those bullets stopped the beating hearts of my son and his wife?

"There are no easy answers to such questions," says John E. Thiel, professor of religious studies at Fairfield University in Fairfield, Connecticut. He points out that "the great Christian thinkers of the past, like St. Augustine, typically explained evil as something God allowed in order to bring a greater good from it. But this explanation can be emotionally difficult for believers, because it means that God directly causes evil to occur." In the final analysis, Professor Thiel acknowledges, "God's ways are mysterious."

Many other professors, philosophers, and theologians have for centuries struggled with the problem of why evil exists, and why it is so powerful, extensive, and destructive. Ultimately, in the words of the late Rev. John Macquarrie, a religion professor under whom, as I mentioned earlier, I was privileged to study at Oxford University, the question comes down to this: "Should one see evil as a challenge which, if we overcome it, adds zest to life in a basically good world? Or should one see life as nightmarish, far beyond human powers to affect?"

Professor John Hick, author of *Evil and the God of Love*, acknowledges "divine permission" when it comes to the suffering caused by evil in this world, because this is necessary for "the spiritual growth of souls." But he admits that there is a serious problem with suffering:

> The problem consists...in the fact that instead of serving a constructive purpose, pain and misery seem to be distributed in random and meaningless ways, with the result that suffering is often undeserved and often falls upon men in amounts exceeding anything that could be rationally intended.

I could certainly relate personally to this problem, remembering that day in 1993 when evil struck me in my gut, my heart, my spirit—one phone call altering my life forever, the phone call telling me that my son John and his wife Nancy had been murdered in the middle of the night as they lay sleeping in their newly purchased home in Bigfork, Montana.

I had to fly to Montana to deal with police and pack up John and Nancy's belongings, most of them still in boxes. I traveled from New York with my sons Paul and Frank supporting me on this terrible journey. When we got to the house, which none of us had yet seen, we went first and immediately to the bedroom of death to pray. We entered and, in shock, felt an indescribable coldness that made us fall to our knees and seek the Lord's help. Our prayer was specifically to beg God to exorcise the evil from that room. For evil was palpably there, devastating and frightful.

Confronting Evil without Finding Answers

I had always wrestled with the undeniable fact that evil exists in this world, but I had never believed that evil was an actual entity. My belief was that it could be defined clearly as "the absence of good." Aristotle, for example, taught that evil has no real existence, but erupts from the bad choices made by humans. St. Augustine said the same thing, only in his own way: "Iniquity is not a substance, but the swerving of the will which is turned towards lower things and away from thee, O Lord, Who art the Supreme Substance." In other words, no being is evil by nature, only by choice. This is what my Catholic education had taught me, and this is what I had always assumed to be true. On that August day, I was no longer so sure.

Within six months I had another chilling experience. I was at the time the executive editor of a Connecticut newspaper and one day a man I didn't know showed up in my office. He was truly a gentleman and said he was from Bigfork, Montana, where my kids had been murdered. Expressing his sorrow, he said he owned the Bigfork Inn and that if ever I needed to go back to that town, I was welcome to be his guest at the inn.

I thanked him, and then he started telling me a story that went like this: "If you were ever to go back to where your son lived, you would find that the area has long been known as 'the place of evil spirits.' The Indians who would

migrate up from the south and down from the north refused to settle in that area, because they believed that evil
spirits were really there." The man reminded me that the
killer, who turned out to be the son of the people from
whom John and Nancy had just bought the house and was
strangely named Joseph "Shadow" Clark, had lived most of
his life in that house, located in the vicinity of this "place of
evil spirits." The implication seemed to clearly be that the
young man may have been in some way connected with this
folkloric evil.

I didn't quite know how to respond, except to thank my
visitor and tell him that I didn't really believe in evil spirits. Still, what he said made an impression on me.

Once again, faced by the enormity of truly horrendous
evil, I found that philosophical explanations fell flat. For
me and for my family, evil would never again be an academic issue. The questions were soul-wrenching: As a family, had we been singled out to be tormented? And, if so, by
whom? Is evil after all an entity? Does it have a name?
Who is Satan, really?

I got so caught up with questions like these that I con-
sulted *Bartlett's Familiar Quotations* just to see what re-
spected people of the past had to say about evil. I was star-
tled when I saw how often the word "evil" had been in the
thoughts of the world's great writers. The book contained
some two hundred quotes from the Bible to the works of
contemporary authors that included the word "evil."
Certainly I could not deny that our world is much affected
by evil and has been since the dawn of creation.

European theologian Hans Küng in his writings has
pointed out that the ancient world was filled with belief in
devils and fear of devils:

People often speculated about whole hierarchies of evil spirits under the leadership of Satan, Belial or Beelzebub... The Old Testament had been very reserved in respect to belief in devils. But between 538 and 331 B.C. Israel belonged to the Persian Empire, with its dualistic religion of a good god from whom all good proceeds, and an evil god, the source of all evil. The influence of this belief is unmistakable...

Fr. Küng then goes on to point out that Jesus has a different message: "He preaches the joyful message of God's rule and not the threatening message of Satan's rule." Of course, none of this really touches on the question of why evil exists and why it is so strong and pervasive. And where is God in all this? How are we to reconcile the existence of a good and loving God with the horror of evil? If God is good, how did vice, ugliness, disorder, suffering, and death become part of the universe he created? If God's character is love, how could he permit the grave harm caused by evil? If God is all-powerful, how could he not destroy evil or, at the very least, limit its scope and power?

Questions like these, of course, are only different ways of wording the problem that theologians, philosophers, priests, and ordinary people have had to confront since the dawn of creation. Many have come to an agreement that perhaps the best understanding of evil can be found in what philosophers call "the free-will defense." As Alvin Plantinga explains in his essay, "God, Evil, and the Metaphysics of Freedom":

Now God can create free creatures, but he cannot cause or determine them to do only what is right.

For if he does so, then they are not significantly free after all; they do not do what is right freely. To create creatures capable of *moral good*, therefore, he must create creatures capable of moral evil; and he cannot leave these creatures *free* to perform evil and at the same time prevent them from doing so...

The fact these free creatures sometimes go wrong, however, counts neither against God's omnipotence nor against his goodness; for he could have forestalled the occurrence of moral evil only by excising the possibility of moral good.

A good friend of mine, the late Msgr. John A. Cass, made a similar point when he said: "Creatures who could not choose their actions would be automatons." And, he asked, "Is man's freedom worth the cost?" implying an "of course" answer. Both his commentary and that of the other philosophers quoted above nicely take care of defining Satan as the good angel who went bad, by choice.

Where Is God When We Face Evil?

Over and over during the past few years I have been challenged by people who have tried to convince me that evil is so powerful that it has to be an entity, or entities—called the Devil, or devils, or Satan, or whatever—roaming around, trying to ensnare us. I don't buy that. If it were true, it would mean that God created this evil entity, and I find that preposterous.

What I do believe is that, in the words of John Carroll University professor Joseph F. Kelly, "Evil exists in the world because of us, not God." As the theologians quoted earlier point out, there is far too much evidence that we were created as free persons, and because we are free, we make choices. I see evil to be a self-centered choice, or an action perpetrated by someone whose brain—or soul—is defective, specifically in its ability to make proper, moral, good, compassionate choices.

Still, the question remains: How could a good God, an omnipotent God, an all-wise God let evil exist in this world? Philosophers and theologians have pondered that question for centuries and no one has ever come up with a truly satisfactory explanation. I have arrived at a point where I believe that the question of why God allows so many of his beloved creatures to be victims of evil may never be permanently put to rest.

I could relate well to a man who told me of his discomfort with attempts at explaining evil. He said a dilemma crops up when we say, "God allows evil." How can such a statement offer any consolation to victims of bombers and murderers? Doesn't that make God selective, manipulative, and uncaring? These are, of course, human questions. In the end, this man concluded, what we have to deal with when we look at God and evil are painful "gaping holes."

I'd say, humanly speaking, he's right. We can put the blame on Satan, but that doesn't answer the question "Why me?" when we are personally hit by evil. Why evil is built into creation, after all the arguments are put on the table and all the philosophical answers are reviewed, remains a mystery. Our mysterious God keeps some answers to himself. We can't make sense of evil. We can only begin by accepting the mystery and, thus, taking a first step toward finding peace.

My life has forced me to confront the work of evil in our lives and in our world, and I have come to believe, without reservation, that the only real understanding of God, good, and evil can come from looking to Jesus. Hans Küng puts it well:

> It is in suffering particularly that God can be shown to be the One whom Jesus proclaimed, as we saw, "the Father of the lost"...As Father of the lost, he is no longer a God transcendent and remote, but a God close to man in incomprehensible goodness, generously and magnanimously pursuing him through history in darkness, futility and meaninglessness, inviting him to dare to hope, mercifully sustaining him even in his remoteness from God ...the God manifested in Jesus is not a cruel, despotic, legal-minded God, but a God encountering man as redeeming love, identifying himself in Jesus with suffering man.

If Jesus gave us no explanation for why evil continues to have power, he did give us a blueprint for dealing with it. "Overcome evil with good," said Jesus, whose own life was violently taken by his enemies.

To accept the advice given by Jesus is, I believe, the only way to flourish in a world where evil, from the beginning, has taken up residence. I know from experience that Jesus' approach, which puts good into practice, is better than getting lost in a web of "gaping holes."

Further, I think that old question of why God permits evil is not really relevant today. I think we have to look at the terribly unequal and unfair distribution of the world's resources to get at the root of why so much hate has surfaced in certain countries. In a powerful book first published more than thirty years ago—*Jesus Before Christianity*—Dominican Fr. Albert Nolan, serving in South Africa, anticipated "catastrophe" and the "escalation of violence."

> More than one billion people . . . experience hunger for at least part of every year . . . They also lack clean water, elementary education and basic health care . . . Only God knows how many millions die of starvation . . . The system was not designed to solve such problems. It can produce more and more wealth, but it is incapable of ensuring that even the bare necessities of life are evenly distributed. This is because it is geared to profits rather than to people.

Fr. Nolan shows brilliantly how Jesus is "the true picture of God," who sent his Son to show us how to "understand the structures of evil in the world as it is today." To believe in Jesus, Fr. Nolan reminds us, is to let go of the hate and fear that keep wars and violence going and "to believe that goodness can and will triumph over evil."

I am reminded of the remarkable Simone Weil, a Jewish philosophy student in Europe in the early World War II years, noted today for her writings and teachings, so Catholic in spirit, who had to deal with evil in her short life. "We cannot contemplate without terror the extent of the evil which man can do and endure," she wrote. And yet, in the midst of the struggle for the survival of spirituality in devastating political times, she concluded that "God is present in extreme evil" through the redemptive suffering of the Cross.

Princeton philosophy professor Diogenes Allen, writing about this Jewish-born French woman who served in the French Resistance and wavered on the brink of Roman Catholicism before her death at age thirty-four in 1943, comments on Simone Weil's a remarkable explanation for suffering endured because of evil:

> Weil claims that in affliction we have the most perfect contact with the love of God that is possible for a human being in this life... Contact with his love can be joyous even in the midst of suffering; for we can receive his gracious presence in the midst of our distress. Finally, it is possible after such a presence is known for a person to be in distress and to recognize the very distress to be itself a contact with the love of God. This is not simply to recognize a gracious presence *through* yielding to suffering; it is to find the distress itself as the touch of his love.

To believe that God is there with us when we have been battered by evil may be one of the most difficult challenges we will ever face. Yet, God *is* there and we can seek him out, but only if we choose the road walked by Jesus, the road with an arrow marked "forgiveness," where we will find the "touch of his love" every step of the way.

And then, in the end, there is an amazing bonus for all in God's creation because of this choice we have made. Through all the pain, through all the suffering, we may never get the completely clear answers we would like, but the fact remains that God will ultimately make all things work together for good.

A new world is born when a wrong is forgiven; and only the power that destroys and creates worlds can cause forgiveness to bloom within the wilderness of life here on earth.

—Joel Marcus

3
HUMAN WAYS VS. JESUS' WAY OF DEALING WITH HURT AND INJUSTICE

Jesus counseled "love your enemies" and then modeled that behavior for his followers. In so doing he revealed the nature of God. Jesus demonstrated that God shows unending, non-coercive patience with humanity . . . The fact that God acts toward humanity in this way and Christ expects us to forgive as God has forgiven us points to a nonviolent way of life as normative for Christ's followers.

—Terrence J. Rynne

After the tragic deaths of my children, Peter, John and Nancy, I spent a lot of time praying and reading the words of great spiritual writers at every free moment I could find. Sometimes even the writings of good people trying to inspire others facing near-impossible struggles only made me feel worse. When I found an old book entitled *No Pat Answers*, I picked it up, because at that point I truly felt there would never be any "pat answers" to explain my losses. The author, Eugenia Price, confirmed that view: "We have to face up to the fact that in all of life with God, there is an area of mystery which we will never be able to understand or solve—at least in this life...Putting one's faith in Jesus Christ in no way guarantees an insurance policy against smashed dreams or blighted expectations." But Jesus is there, she adds, noting that "Jesus is in this thing with us. He will prompt us, but he has to get our attention first." Rather cynically, I silently muttered that he had my attention, but not my understanding.

I happened then to read *Broken Vessels*, written by the late Andre Dubus, a critically acclaimed writer, a Catholic believer who after being struck by a car in 1986 became permanently disabled. One of his essays contained these lines:

> After the dead are buried, and the maimed have left the hospitals and started their new lives, after the physical pain of grief has become, with time, a permanent wound in the soul, a sorrow that will last as long as the body does, after the horrors become nightmares and sudden daylight memories, then comes the transcendent and common bond of human suffering, and with that comes forgiveness, and with forgiveness comes love.

I wanted so much to believe the truth of his words, but I related more to what the great British statesman Edmund Burke had written after the death of his son in 1794:

> I live in an inverted order. They who ought to have succeeded me, have gone before me. They, who

should have been to me as posterity, are in the place of ancestors. The storm has gone over me; and I lie like one of those old oaks which the late hurricane hath scattered about me...I am torn up by the roots, and lie prostrate on the earth! There, and prostrate there, I must unfeignedly recognize the divine justice and in some degree submit to it.

In that dark place where I kept finding myself, I was battling, trying hard to hold on constructively to all I had ever believed about forgiveness. Most times I would say I could "forgive," but in between those times everything I did at work, at home, or with my family would be in stark remembrance of Peter, John, and Nancy and their tragic deaths. I wanted to get to the place of which the New England preacher Henry Ward Beecher had spoken:

I can "forgive but I can't forget," is another way of saying "I will not forgive." Forgiveness ought to be like a canceled note, torn in two and burnt up so that it can never be shown against the man.

Then came a Tuesday night in December 1993 that I shall never forget. I had been watching the late news on television, appalled at what I was seeing. People were milling around at a railroad train stopped at a station on Long Island, all of them in a state of shock. Unfolding before them was a tragic scene, with dead and wounded people being taken off the train. A man had apparently boarded the train in New York City carrying a 9-millimeter gun armed with a 15-round magazine. During the train trip he had suddenly opened fire, shooting people sitting peace-fully on their way home from work.

By the time his fury was spent, the man, later identified as thirty-five-year-old Colin Ferguson, had killed five peo-ple and injured twenty others. It was a totally senseless massacre. All the bystanders, voicing their reactions as tel-evision microphones were being shoved in their faces, ex-pressed the same feelings—hate for the killer and a desire for revenge.

I was undergoing an enormous emotional reaction as I watched, because only four months earlier I had gotten the tragic news of the murder of my son John and his wife Nancy by an intruder wielding a 9-millimeter gun. The killer had not been found. If ever he were to be found, I wondered, how would I react? As I struggled with my own anger and devastation, I asked myself: Would I be filled with hate, like the people I was watching on TV, when that phantom killer became a person with a face and a name?

I didn't have to contemplate that question very long. For just at that moment, as I was watching the Long Island Railroad massacre, my phone rang. It was Montana's Lake County sheriff, Joe Geldrich, calling me from that state, twenty-five hundred miles away from where I live. "I have some news for you," he said. "We caught the killer of your son and daughter-in-law."

What he went on to say stunned me. The "killer," he explained, was the eighteen-year-old son of Mr. and Mrs. Joseph Clark, the people from whom John and Nancy had bought their home only a few months earlier. His name was Joseph "Shadow" Clark and he was a first-year student at a Quaker college in Oregon. They had found "Shadow," the name by which he was known, because he had started talking to some fellow students about having killed two people. The students reported this to the administrators, who then went to the police.

I kept interrupting the sheriff, wanting to know why this boy—whom he described as "an honor student and a Fundamentalist Christian"—had killed my kids. Joe Geldrich didn't know. Shadow Clark never did say why— neither then nor after. As the case turned out, he entered a plea and got life imprisonment with no parole until he's sixty years old, but he never revealed his motive for killing two beautiful people.

On that December night, I was utterly devastated. Torment siezed my soul as I visualized this Shadow Clark creeping up to the bedroom with that deadly gun. I shivered from the sense of evil that seeped out of that image. I had been grappling with the words of Jesus—that we must forgive those who do us harm—ever since I had gotten the dreadful news of the murders. I had always been able to forgive those who had hurt me in the past. But this was different. This person had killed my son and daughter-in-law, and had seared me and my remaining five children with a pain that would endure forever. Now I had his name and would see his face. Could I forgive him?

Seeking Forgiveness though Lost in Darkness

This question tore me apart, and for many weeks it surged up through my prison of anger, pain, desolate sadness, and beautiful memories of John and Nancy. It frightened me. I felt uncertain as to where I was, and whether I could come to accept the limitless forgiveness commanded by Jesus. I wondered if I would become hardened by this brutal crime, even as I remembered another plea from the Bible, "Harden not your hearts."

I started to meet with other crime victims, asking if they could forgive those who had so hurt them. Most of them couldn't get over their anger. As I listened, I realized why they wanted to remain angry. Anger made them feel powerful; it was their weapon against the criminal. Some expressed the fear that to forgive would mean they were weaklings, soft on criminals. I could see what some of them couldn't—that their anger was keeping them locked in hate, eating away at them, eroding their souls. When I would turn on the television news and hear about killings and retaliations between different groups—the Serbs and the Muslims in Bosnia, the Arabs and Jews in Israel—I would strongly feel that I was hearing the same message: that we hang on to hate in order to feel powerful, that it is some kind of compensation for our lost power. It was all so obviously wrong, and so contradictory to the message of Christ.

Even as I was struggling with my personal loss, I was beginning to see more clearly what happens to people who can't let go of their pain at having suffered an injustice, and I didn't want that fate for myself. These people were letting something from the past pollute their present, and they were unaware of how they were being psychologically and spiritually damaged by this. Over the millennia, the wise have understood that, as Confucius put it, "To be wronged is nothing unless you continue to remember it."

Yet, we all too often let the hurts we have suffered take root in us, crowding out everything else in our hearts. And we

have been socialized to value revenge, with influences rang-
ing from the "cowboy and Indian" movies we saw as kids, to
the constant wars, to the pro–death penalty stance that has always charateized this country. Add to this the fact that, given
our human nature, forgiving someone who has hurt us is one
of the hardest things to do. I can still recall my father's Italian
friends saying that forgiveness is not a sign of weakness, that
being able to forgive means you have a strong soul. Yet, in
practice, if anyone hurt them, they would "even the score," to
use their words. We all want an "eye for an eye," because that
makes us feel powerful. And thus, forgiving remains alien to
us who so love to "even the score." We blind ourselves to the
truth that, as Carl Jung said, "You always become the thing
you fight the most." He wasn't the only one to point out the
fact that we become what we hate.

Not only people, but nations, too, become what they
hate, says theology professor Walter Wink in his important
book, *Engaging the Powers*. He quotes George William
Russell, author of *Evil and World Order*, who writes, "By in-
tensity of hatred, nations create in themselves the charac-
teristics they imagine in their enemies." Professor Wink
adds that "we want desperately to believe that our forcible
retaliation to evil is like a projectile fired from a gun that
will drop evil in its tracks. In fact, it is more like a ball
thrown by a pitcher that will, as likely as not, carom back
at us, or over the fence."

Imagine what would happen if all nations followed the
teaching of Christ to love their enemies. It would be love
that would be fired, and it would be love that would "carom
back at us." The world would be radically transformed as
love ended national and international conflicts fueled by

greed and the desire for power. Then peace would reign. This is a message our late holy father Pope John Paul II tried to get across to leaders of the world's nations.

Conquering the Desire for Revenge

I had long been praying that the sword of sorrow that Shadow Clark had pierced me with would not destroy my soul with hatred or a desire for revenge, and the Lord was hearing my prayer. I was beginning to understand where forgiveness must begin—by putting the spotlight on ourselves to reveal who we really are when we become the victim of brutal evil or even of lesser crimes, of assaults to our ego or any kind of abuse directed at us.

I have seen people stay locked into their hurts from insults by family members, from "downsizing" by an employer, from lawsuits against them and all kinds of other injustices, both perceived and real. But I have also seen nobility shine forth from people who have suffered severe hurt and loss. One such person was a rabbi whose entire family had been killed in the Holocaust. After he managed to get to America, he said he had forgiven Hitler. A reporter asked him how he could forgive someone who had done so much terrible harm to him and others. The rabbi answered, "I forgave Hitler—because I did not want to bring him to America with me." The wisdom of his words struck me deeply, and I was awed by his ability to free himself from hate and conflict and turmoil. He underscored for me the human value of forgiveness, the fact that holding onto anger, hate, and vengeance destroys any possibility of finding peace.

The day I got a call from a reporter asking me how I felt about the murderer of my children, I remember responding instinctively, with two words: "Incredibly sad." That's when I knew I had begun to forgive. I was utterly saddened to think of an eighteen-year-old who had permanently altered so many lives and destroyed three, those of John, Nancy, and himself. I had started to pray for Shadow Clark, that he could respond to God's grace and be redeemed. I was learning that I had the power to forgive, to not let an assassin destroy who I am or to put a wedge between me and my God.

This didn't mean that my anger was gone or that I didn't want the murderer severely punished. I would not be human if I were to retreat from the need to confront evil in order to overcome it. But confronting and overcoming evil is not the same as revenge. The final chapter in any tragedy must never be revenge or the mistake of throwing away other human beings because we consider them worthless, unredeemable, or unloved by God.

The Great Paradox of Forgiveness

Therein is the greatest paradox of all—that God loves both—both the one who is hurt and the one who does the hurting. This is hard to understand, but it is the truth. As Professor Walter Wink writes,

> We are to love our enemies, says Jesus, because God does. God makes the "sun rise on the evil and on the good and sends rain on the righteous and on the unrighteous" (Matt. 5:45) ...

Jesus' laconic mention of God's all inclusive parental care is thus charged with an unexpected consequence for human behavior: we can love our enemies, because God does. If we wish to correspond to the central reality of the universe, we will behave as God behaves—and God embraces all, evenhandedly. This radical vision of God, already perceived by the Hebrew prophets...is the basis for true human community.

Then Professor Wink adds words that should give us pause:

If, however, we believe that the God who loves us hates those whom we hate, we insert an insidious doubt into our own lives. Unconsciously we know that a deity hostile towards others is potentially hostile to us as well. And we know, better than anyone, that there is plenty of cause for such hostility. If God did not send sun and rain on everyone equally, God would not only not love everyone, but love no one.

These words have powerful implications globally. If ever we are to have peace in this world, it must begin with the recognition that we need to change a long-established mindset that makes people of one country adversaries of another. We have to stop thinking of others as enemies and start seeing them as truly our kin. Only then can we acknowledge that they are loved by God just as we are, and that we should all be cherishing one another.

In an astounding book called *The Nonviolent Coming of God*, James Douglass maintains that when Christ said "Love your enemies," it was to give us not "an impossible demand, but a way of saving us from our righteousness and from our self-destructive, world-destructive violence." Jesuit Fr. William Reiser, through the lens of theology, affirms that forgiving our enemies means feeling toward the world "as God himself does."

These passages reinforce what I learned long ago, that the words most often used by Jesus in his ministry were "forgiveness" and "mercy." Jesus acknowledged that what he was asking of us was not easy. He taught us by his words and his life that to follow him—to be a Christian—meant that we had to be different. We had to give up the self-centered life in which ego is supreme and take on the hard task of being transformed into the image of the Son of God. Central to his message was getting across to us that being like him meant we would be a contradiction to the world, especially in embracing his bottom-line teaching to "overcome evil with good"—another way of saying "forgive."

To forgive is just what the word itself says—to offer a gift before it's been earned or even deserved. That's how God treats us, and that's why forgiving is so difficult, because it is acting as God would. It doesn't mean giving in; it means letting go. If we don't forgive, we stay emotionally handcuffed to the person—or the nation—that hurt us. And if we're handcuffed, we are not free, never at peace, never able to do God's work. Forgiveness is a boomerang—the gift we send out is what we're going to get back.

After I wrote *The Pummeled Heart*, where I focused on my journey to find forgiveness for Peter for his self-inflicted death, and forgiveness for the eighteen-year-old stranger who had murdered my son John and his wife Nancy, my world changed. I was a bit naïve, never expecting that some people would respond negatively to my belief in the importance of forgiveness. All too many were like Edna, who contacted me after reading my book to say she could not understand how I could go on day after day not hating the young man who had murdered my son and daughter-in-law. Her daughter had been murdered by a man who had strangled her and dumped her body in a waste disposal bin. She wrote that she thought of this crime day and night. She hated the killer. She wanted him to get the death penalty.

Of course, I could understand her anger. My empathy for her and her family was immense. Nothing quite matches the agony of losing a child. Someone once said "The death of a child is an impossible grief," and that is so true because there are in fact no words for such a loss. But I was learning that if you hang on to the anger and bitterness caused by a horrendous crime, the one being hurt is you. I tried to get Edna to see that her anger was giving new power to the murderer, for now he was killing her, too, little by little. And, sadly, she was letting her pain eat the goodness out of her. She stopped calling me or answering my phone calls.

But then there were other people who contacted me, not to express anger or to blast me for being naïve or wrong, but to thank me for having helped them see the healing power of forgiveness, like the mother who had somehow found my phone number and called me from a southern state far distant from my own. She thanked me for having "saved" her life. Her son, too, had committed suicide and she had turned this tormenting pain inward, blaming herself for his death. She had, in her agony, believed that she was the one deserving of death, and so planned to kill herself—until she read of Peter's suicide in another of my books. She then came to see that if I could survive this horror, so could she.

I told her that Peter had left us a "Dear Family..." letter on tape and I read some of this to her to help her better understand the internal tragedy a son might be experiencing that would make him take his life. Peter wanted us to know what had been going on in his tortured brain since his teen years, even as he was getting the best medical care I could find for him after he was diagnosed as mentally ill by psychiatrists at Stony Brook University Hospital on Long Island. With different doctors and different treatment, we believed Peter would get the "healing" he needed. He did so much good work in the next ten years, completing a two-year tour in the U.S. Army, finishing college, teaching math at a Catholic school in Guam, writing three anti-war books for major publishers. But he was never healed. His illness, instead, became focused on the evil and suffering in this world. He became particularly obsessed with the torments inflicted on people by war.

When the Gulf War began in January 1991, Peter lost all "natural instinct" to stay alive, he told us in the tape he left us. But he also had his own explanation for where this death choice came from, for he said he was "born with a missing part": "My life is like a Rolls Royce, without spark plugs. It looks great, but it has a hidden flaw that keeps it from running properly. The absence of that spark has often made even the simplest setbacks for me almost unendurable..."

My caller cried on the phone, telling me that now she had a better understanding of why her son's pain was "unendurable." Having made the choice not to take her own life, she could now truly forgive her son.

After Injustice, We Are in Charge of Our Choices

Certainly, we had very much in common, for both of us had learned that, yes, this kind of pain takes up permanent residence in a person. But I had learned and wanted to pass on that there is only one person in charge of damage control, and that is ourselves.

Pain can't stop you from growing, working, and loving unless you let it. You are the one with the choices. Stay bitter and angry and you give your pain the power to destroy you. If you can't let go of your feelings of rage, you will be stuck in a never-ending internal war.

I so clearly understood this, and thanks be to God, because of my Christian faith, I knew there was only one place where I could find the specific inspiration that would make me capable of genuine forgiveness. I went to Jesus. Yet, in blunt honesty, I have to admit that I was then in a fragile state. I knew that if I were to be hurt again by one of the world's jagged edges, I could be lost.

That's why I then sought and still now continually seek help from good people who are my brothers and sisters in pain—from the centuries past to the present—and I do, truly, find it. Consider Dietrich Bonhoeffer, one of the strongest leaders of the resistance against the evil of Hitler's regime. Bonhoeffer was executed for his devotion to God, his church, his friends, and his pre-Hitler country. He asked, "If you want to connect more deeply with God, is that possible if you have unforgiveness in your heart?...An unforgiving heart is blocked from listening to God...and there is no freedom when the heart and soul and mind are unforgiving, and, so, trapped."

Then he wrote that there is a relationship between forgiveness and grace—grace, which great preachers have called "God's footprints in our soul." Bonhoeffer was an innocent man of God about to be executed, yet could write what he saw was the truth—that God's footsteps can't be felt when a soul is unforgiving.

I discovered so many great teachers like him, people who did more than talk the talk. They lived by the forgiveness they knew was essential—for no one becomes a disciple, let alone an image, of God's Son, the Lord Jesus, without forgiving.

An eye for an eye makes the whole world blind.
                                        —Mohandas Gandhi

4
WHEN THE HEART BLOCKS FORGIVENESS

When we are crushed like grapes, we cannot think of the wine we will become.

—Henri J. M. Nowen

Consider the story of Sweeney Todd. Set in London, with a backdrop befitting a Charles Dickens story, this is perhaps the darkest tale ever to be presented with artistry on Broadway and in the movies. Sweeney, a barber, is a crime victim, sent to Australia by an evil judge who plans to abduct Sweeney's wife and daughter for his own sexual gratification. Sweeney serves fifteen years at hard labor before he can escape and return to London—vowing revenge.

Anyone who goes to the theatre or the movies has probably seen *Sweeney Todd* and knows the rest of the story. Sweeney makes people *pay* for what happened to him and his family—and it doesn't matter that they may be innocent citizens of London, merely wanting a shave and a haircut.

He butchers them and then bakes their flesh into meat pies, with the help of a female accomplice.

This brutality for the sake of revenge is, indeed, a moral crime. But there is also a psychological explanation for such hate-in-action. It is called "redirected aggression." Sadly, we can encounter this not only on the stage and screen but in our own lives as well.

I remember reading a letter to the editor in my local newspaper after President George Bush launched the Iraq war in response to the attack of 9/11, having convinced many Americans that Saddam Hussein and his people were responsible for this tragedy. The letter was written by a man in his eighties, a World War II veteran, and he was livid that some people were opposed to our government's Iraq war. "We were attacked—and *somebody has to pay,*" he wrote.

Guilt and responsibility didn't matter to this man. It was simply that *"somebody"* had to pay—and that is where "redirected aggression" comes in, based on the view that for some "crimes," forgiveness is weakness and stupidity. Revenge—of any kind—is justified.

"When an individual suffers pain, he most often responds by passing it on to someone else. When possible, that someone else is the perpetrator, the original source of the pain. But if this cannot be achieved, then others are liable to be victimized, regardless of innocence," writes Professor David P. Barash, author of *Natural Selections: Selfish Altruists, Honest Liars, and Other Realities of Evolution.* He explains this "redirected aggression—the passing of pain from one victim to another," as not being "merely the stuff of literature and drama."

…sadly, the urge to pass along pain lurks behind modern warfare not less than it did behind medieval pageantry, leaving its mark in the genocidal wars of the 20th century as well as those that threaten to overwhelm the 21st. It underlies many of the most prominent, enduring themes of literature, history, anthropology, psychology and religion. It haunts our criminal courts, our streets, our battle fields, our homes, our hearts. There is nothing new about the phenomenon…

Professor Barash then considers "redirected aggression" from the perspective of the Christian tradition, saying,

In a masterpiece of painfully accurate revelation, G. K. Chesterton once wrote that Christianity hasn't been tried and found wanting; rather, it has been found difficult and left untried. Never has that been more true than in cases of personal pain and our reaction to it. Thus, Jesus urged us to love our enemies, and if slapped, turn the other cheek. But for millennia —before Jesus and after—human beings and their animal brethren have been far more likely to respond to pain and injury with a retaliating barrage of the same sort, generating yet more injury and pain…

Fr. Robert Barron, author of *The Strangest Way: Walking the Christian Path*, explains this well:

The old schemas of handling disorder through vengeance restored a tentative and very unreliable

"peace," which was really nothing but a pause between conflicts. Evil met with evil only intensifies,
just as fire met with fire only increases the heat...

On the Cross, the Son of God took on the hatred of all us sinners, and in his forgiving love, he
took that hatred away. By creating a way out of the
net of our sinfulness, by doing what no mere
philosopher, poet, politician, or social reformer
could possibly do, Jesus saved us.

We may intellectually know the truth of these words,
but when we are hit with the unspeakable—with that which
causes us to scream out "Why?"—it is inevitable that we become overwhelmed by anger, turning our wrath at God for
not having prevented the horrible events that have caused
us the pain we are experiencing. And our very human reaction is to want revenge, most often defined as "justice."

As I am writing this, I have before me a story in today's
newspaper telling of the brutal murder of a New York city
woman, Adrienne Shelly, age forty, an actress and a mother.
An intruder, Diego Pillco, had followed her into her apart-
ment to rob her, and then accidentally knocked her unconscious. Fearful of what would happen to him if she revived
and made a complaint against him, he choked her and
hanged her by a sheet tied to the shower rod in the bathroom. Another horrendous horror story.

The judge acknowledged that he could offer no comfort to the family and he let the murdered woman's husband, Andrew Ostroy, speak. In his anger Mr. Ostroy, looking directly at the killer, called him "an animal and a beast"
for having taken the life of "a loving woman who, unlike

you, had so much to give to society...I want you to suffer like she suffered, to live a life of fear, the same fear she felt when she realized she was about to die."

Then this father, looking directly at the killer, spoke of his daughter, saying, "You sentenced that little girl to a lifetime of sadness and questions and feelings of what could've been..."

I have met with many people who, like Mr. Ostroy and myself, were thrust into a new and disturbing life because a loved one was killed at the hands of another human person. And I have asked myself: How can one talk forgiveness to someone so traumatized by the pain of losing a loved one in so terrible a way? I remember the sad words of a mother whose daughter was killed by her husband. Unable to forgive her son-in-law, who had asked her forgiveness, this mother, in anguish, told her minister that she feared the killer would one day die and go to heaven and be with her daughter, while she would be in hell because she could not forgive him. I heard this with such sadness, knowing the pain and devastation this mother was living with.

No one gets through life without suffering from wrongs, some from another's selfishness, some from outright injustice. "Hurts and transgressions are as different as the people who commit them, but all result from living in a community and all cause emotional pain," writes Fr. Rick Potts, editor of *Liguorian* magazine. He continues:

> And how do we deal with that pain? Our first response is usually to get revenge, or at least justice. But our most common reaction is to grab hold of the pain and refuse to let go...

We wrap our pain in a mantle of justice and guard it carefully. We nurture and feed it, allowing it to ferment and grow—the bigger to clobber someone over the head with...It takes effort and time to heal, to come to the forgiveness that is fundamental to our faith...This is not an easy thing to do...It requires the death of our anger, it requires letting go of the past, it requires turning over our pain to the Lord and choosing life and love.

I have often been criticized, even made fun of, because I write of forgiveness and work against the killing of killers via the death penalty, which is still the way we in most of the United States punish people convicted of the crime of murder. In one of the many letters I have received over the years, a Texas Catholic mother wrote:

I admire your spirit of forgiveness and wish I could emulate you. However I feel it raises some questions.

Isn't our liberal system towards criminals already too much based on forgiveness, permitting them to avoid completing their term in prison or avoid it entirely, letting them loose on the streets again, free to commit more crimes?

Isn't there a correlation between forgiveness on the injured party's side and blindness to responsibility and consequences on the criminal side?

I wish for a society with more peace, less violence and I am not sure at this stage in our society unconditional forgiveness is the answer. Also, how would you carry through that personal decision to our legal and penal system?

I have a five-year-old daughter and a two-year-old son and when I think of the brutal murder of the two year old boy in England last year, I cannot in my heart believe I could forgive the perpetrators if my children were the victims of the same anguish, terror and finally senseless killing as that poor innocent child. It is evil in its purest form and I am not sure I can forgive evil, nor whether I am required to.

I feel there should be an order in society and forgiveness in such circumstances makes a travesty of the order that decent, law-abiding, Christian-values-respecting people try to maintain and build upon. *Let God forgive.* Let *citizens* demonstrate that there are consequences to evil acts and a price to pay. As for the Christian in his/her personal life, let him/her not be an accomplice to perpetuating a system that coddles criminals and ignores victims...

This was a difficult letter to answer, because the mother was saying much I understood and agreed with. I responded, underscoring the fact that, that like her, I do not believe in unconditional forgiveness, if by that one means letting a criminal get away with a crime. People must not get away with hurting others. But forgiveness, I emphasized, means something else. I think it means not letting ourselves get stuck on anger or vengeance, which then only hurts us more. I think forgiveness also means that we should remember everyone comes from God, and so we are all connected. Doesn't this imply that we should still care for the person, while we hate the crime? I think when Jesus said "overcome evil with good," it was to impress upon us that every soul is worth being saved.

Yet, in all honesty, I know how difficult it is to even to think about forgiveness when we are utterly devastated, having been wounded by an unexpected and unthinkable blow. This is especially the case with people who have had to bury a loved one who has died as a result of suicide. Such people often find themselves in tormenting pain, trying to understand why someone they loved gave up on life. The anguish of suicide defies explanation. I have spoken with so many family members left to deal with their bafflement, pain, guilt, anger, and questions after the suicide of a loved one. "It feels like a betrayal. Wasn't our love good enough?" asked the sister of a young man who was a Gulf War veteran. After the funeral, she said, "The pain was so intense, I didn't know what to do with it. I didn't believe I could still live with this much pain."

Another woman, whose thirty-one-year-old brother committed suicide, recalled spending the entire first year after his death feeling "totally alone. I had anger, guilt, sadness, rage, and so many 'whys?'—it was a constant obsession. It was my silent, dirty, shameful secret. Because I was so mixed up, I felt like I was going crazy." Fortunately, she found a group called Survivors of Suicide, where people could come together and share thoughts and feelings similar to her own.

Knowing she wasn't alone was the beginning of her healing, even while she still had to deal with sudden bouts of sadness and anger that her beloved brother had made the choice to leave them. Understanding came slowly, but she learned, as Dr. John Jordan, who has researched suicide survivors, has said, that "if you have a loved one murdered, you feel rage at the perpetrator. But the problem is that in suicide, the perpetrator is also the victim."

Grappling with the "Betrayal" of Suicide

The searing pain that accompanies the issue of betrayal is experienced by every family that has had to deal with the suicide of a loved one. I remember reading a book entitled *The Sacred Journey* that I picked up at a book sale shortly after my own son Peter's suicide in 1991. It had been written by Frederick Buechner, a Presbyterian minister in Vermont. As I began reading the book, I was struck by his words that "even in the most humdrum of our days, God speaks." But a few paragraphs later, I was jolted, as I read, "But what is God saying through a good man's suicide?"

Indeed, the author's father had committed suicide and Rev. Buechner, still a child then, would for the rest of his life remember the day when the world that had seemed so good to him "had come to an end." And he wrote, "When somebody you love dies, Mark Twain said, it is like when your house burns down; it isn't for years that you realize the full extent of your loss."

Frederick, the boy, was told by his grandmother that he had to "face reality." She added that you have to "grit your teeth and clench your fists in order to survive the world at its harshest and worst..." But he was to go on to learn that "the trouble with steeling yourself against the harshness of reality is that the same steel that secures your life against being destroyed secures your life also against being opened up and transformed by the holy power that life itself comes from. You can survive on your own," he continues. "You can even prevail on your own. But you cannot become human on your own...the one thing a clenched fist cannot do is accept, even from *le bon Dieu* himself, a helping hand."

The "clenched fist" keeps out, most of all, forgiveness.

If there is one situation that forces you to look at where you really stand with regard to forgiveness, it certainly is suicide. I start each day with a prayer for my son Peter, never for a moment being able to forget the morning of March 18, 1991, when at the age of twenty-seven, he walked to a pond about a mile from our home where he used to go to meditate, and put a bullet through his head.

I am more fortunate than many survivors of suicide victims because Peter left us several notes, and, out of kindness, something more—a lengthy taped message to try to help us understand. His beginning words probably apply to all adult suicides—

> Dear Family: Why? That must be the question on your mind right now. I don't know really, not for sure. Obviously, there's been some combination of chronic psychological problems which have culminated in my own self-destruction. Yet, it's difficult for me to put my finger on the complex, probably subconscious emotions that make me feel suicidal. Even if I could pin them down inside me, it's doubtful that I could articulate them...I am in death what I was in life...an enigma to those around me and to myself...

I can't say I ever saw Peter as an "enigma." He was an achiever, brilliant and beautiful, popular with all who went to school with him, worked with him, dealt with him in any way. What comes through in Peter's tape is his agonizing struggle to survive in those times when he felt he was not fully equipped to handle life as it is must be lived on this earth.

Something in the deep-down, crucial, essential mechanism that one needs to greet, and not just endure, each day was missing, and it caused him unrelenting, unbearable pain.

The American Association of Suicidology has coined a word to express this: "psych-ache." I feel that it is this pain, which is so beyond definition, that may be what defeats those adults who, like Peter, are not really on a self-destructive path, yet kill themselves. Many of them are highly intelligent and have attractive personalities. They are creative and outgoing, sensitive, dedicated, and deeply concerned for others. They are also very good at hiding their pathological breakdowns—the terrifying inner turmoil that can usually be kept under control but suddenly and unexpectedly erupts, set off by something that is devastatingly traumatic for them. That something shatters the connection to their carefully crafted safety nets, and they want out of this life.

The survivors are all too often left with what one mother of a twenty-five-year-old son, dead from a self-injected dose of heroin, said was "forever remembering the day that changed our whole life, knowing we'd never be the same again." She was tormented by anger, and worse, the pain of not being able to forgive her son for what he had done to her and the family.

For us, the pain of losing Peter was compounded by where we were and what we had been doing the day before his suicide. Our family had been having the greatest celebration imaginable—the baptism of my daughter Mary's baby, Sophia. Peter was the godfather. In agonizing pain, Mary struggled also with her anger. In her words . . .

The night of my baby's christening I sank into bed with a rare feeling of wholeness, basking in the peace and security of what had seemed a perfect day. Sophia's baptism had been shared that morning by family and a loving church community. My brother Peter was my daughter's godfather. But, shortly after midnight, as I slept happily, Pete walked to the old swamp in back of my mother's house and put a bullet through his head.

The wake-up call, that news-breaking, heart-ripping telephone call, filled me with a pain so excruciating I thought I'd never stand up again. It took about a week after my brother's suicide for anger to set in. It came and went. Sometimes I'd scream curses to the empty air as if the wind would carry my rage to him. How could you do this to me? How could you betray our friendship and trample on my love for you? How could you have tarnished the memory of my baby's christening? How could you be so selfish?

But then my heart moved to Peter's agony. He had suffered acute anxiety for thirteen hellish years. He'd served in the military, finished college, taught school at home and abroad, and written three books. He'd searched courageously and creatively to find a place in the world, but a pervasive and inexplicable shame followed him everywhere. He despised himself for his failures and for his existence. Therapy had never helped and probably never would have. Pete was too complex, too confused, too passionate, too wounded and too sensitive. There was no slot on earth into which he could have fit neatly, and he couldn't accept the idea of a life on the fringe of society without a respectable position at its center.

It's very hard for a suicide survivor to believe that anyone's pain could justify that fatal, irreversible act. I myself wouldn't have been able to believe it if I hadn't been so close to suicide myself when I was younger. I'll never understand why I kept living, but I know what helped turn my life around. I had an epiphany experience; from nowhere I felt God freely give me the grace with which I could begin to forgive myself for being alive.

To forgive is just what the word itself says, to offer a gift before it's been earned or deserved. Pete never had that experience in his heart. He never gave that gift to himself. The least I can do is offer him my forgiveness now, because I remember his pain and I love him so much.

Because I have written about forgiveness as the mother of a suicide victim and a son and daughter-in-law murdered by an intruder in their home, it is not surprising to me that I have been strongly criticized by people who have been deeply hurt and want nothing to do with forgiveness. When they speak to me, I know by their tone of voice why they would shut me out. They are too angry to let go of their belief about punishment for perceived ills, or for the pain they carry inside them as a result of whatever abuse they experienced.

Not Surrendering to Anger

Fr. Robert Barron writes about how easy it would have been for the Rev. Martin Luther King "to have surrendered to sinful anger, given the history of hatred that his people had lived through." After his home had been attacked, "King informed an angry crowd of blacks who had gathered for vengeance that they must love their persecutors even as they hate what they have done." Fr. Barron indicates that this great man saw the sin of anger to be "the lust for vengeance untethered to reason." He goes on to say that

> in Ireland, Rwanda, the Holy Land, Indonesia, China, Russia, the United States—anger is passed on from generation to generation like a bacillus. Never forgetting, never forgiving, never recovering from past offences, people around the globe allow their lust for vengeance to well up unchecked.
>
> And the same phenomenon can be seen in families and communities where grudges are borne for decades, even when the originating offence is long forgotten...

I will never forget the hate I saw in the face of a man who came up to me after I had given a talk on the need for forgiveness if we are to be followers of Christ. His face rigid with fury, he said to me, "So, your son was murdered and you can forgive the killer. But what if your son was the one who did the killing, would you ever forgive him for that?" Before I could respond, he said, "That's what I live with. My son killed a man. I'll never forgive him!"

There is no comfort for someone living with that kind of dark and blinding grief. There is no freedom when the heart blocks forgiveness.

Forever Challenged to "Drink the Cup"

"Can we embrace fully the sorrows" that come to us, unexpected and unwanted? That's the question Fr. Henri J. M. Nouwen dealt with before his death in 1996. He revealed some of his own pain in a book with a title that uses the words of Jesus' own question to his disciples: *Can You Drink the Cup?* This is the question that is asked of all who are now or will ever become Jesus' followers. "It is the question that will have a different meaning every day of our lives," Fr. Nouwen wrote.

Then this priest, who had shared his life with people afflicted with mental disabilities, went on to speak personally not only about the ills that can block forgiveness of God and others, but of what he had learned:

> Joys are hidden in sorrows! I know this from my own times of depression. I know it from living with people with mental handicaps. I know it from looking into the eyes of patients, and from being with the poorest of the poor. We keep forgetting this truth and become overwhelmed by our own darkness. We easily lose sight of our joys and speak of our sorrows as the only reality there is...

We need to be able to let our tears flow freely, tears of sorrow as well as tears of joy, tears that are as rain on the dry ground...

When we lift our cup to life, we must dare to say: "I am grateful for all that has happened to me and led me to this moment." This gratitude which embraces all of our past is what makes our life a true gift for others, because this gratitude erases bitterness, resentments, regret, and revenge as well as all jealousies and rivalries.

This gratitude of which Fr. Nouwen speaks has a name: forgiveness. As we drink we taste our cup, filled now with the sweetness of good wine. And the important thing to remember is that this cup is the cup that Jesus himself drank. It is Jesus himself who gives us the strength to drink it. If we say yes, then we accept the crushing of the grapes because of the sweetness of the reward, *his wine.*

Day after day we are covered with various kinds of dirtiness, with empty words, with prejudices...falsehoods. All this darkens and contaminates our soul. We must wash each other's feet also in the sense that we pardon each other anew. Don't let rancor toward each other poison our soul.

　　　　　—Pope Benedict XVI, washing the feet of priests
　　　　　Holy Thursday, 2008

5

HOW FORGIVENESS FREES
THE HEART, MIND,
BODY, AND SOUL

*He who wishes to revenge injuries by reciprocal hatred will
live in misery. But he who endeavors to drive away hatred
by means of love, fights with pleasure and confidence...
love tends to beget love, so that his hatred disintegrates
and loses force.*

—Baruch Spinoza

A noteworthy study on forgiveness was done at the
University of Michigan's Institute of Social Research
in 2001, a year that was particularly difficult for me as it
marked the tenth anniversary of my son Peter's death by
suicide. The study showed that almost 75 percent of the
participating adults said they were confident that God
had forgiven them for any past wrongdoing. But then
the participants went on to admit, with remarkable honesty, that they themselves were much less able to forgive
others.

The researchers suspected that this admission stemmed from a belief that since God is perfect, he forgives unendingly, whereas we, imperfect ones, find it hard to let bygones be bygones. I had flashbacks, remembering the insensitive question all too many people had asked me after hearing about Peter's death—"How can you forgive your son for his suicide?" Sadder still was the experience I had many times in giving talks about how to survive a "pummeled heart," when someone would angrily state that he or she had a "right" to be unforgiving. I heard their stories—

> "I'll never forgive my sister or talk to her again. She stole my boyfriend."

> "My boss stole my ideas and good work and cheated me out of a promotion and a raise. I'll hate him forever."

> "I raised a son to be a good person. But he became a thief and carried a gun, and one day he killed someone. How could I ever forgive him? I can't."

> "So you can forgive the person who murdered your son and his wife! How can you be so unfeeling? All I can say is that you couldn't have loved them. If you did, you would have made sure the killer got the death penalty. He deserves to die, painfully!"

In all honesty, I could understand their reactions, even as I disagreed with them. For, as I mentioned earlier, I had learned that forgiveness is not a one-time decision. Some days I would find myself actually screaming in fury because three loved ones had died violently. Where was God when my children needed his help? I would find myself shouting these words in an empty room. I was also learning that to forgive involves making a radical decision to live as Jesus taught us, even as we feared that his "limitless" forgiveness was an impossible command.

I also was learning that, because my broken heart would never fully heal and I knew I would experience the pain of it for the rest of my life, I would never be able to say I "forgave" those who had caused such pain, and even God, who had allowed it, and be done with it. No. Every single day I would have to renew my willingness to forgive, and I wouldn't be able to do this on my own, but only with God's help. If Jesus had a goal, it had to be that he was here to help all people see everything as God sees it.

This was confirmed in many of the spiritual books I had begun to read. I was especially helped by the words written in the mid–twentieth century by a biblical scholar, Harry Emerson Fosdick:

> Love even when hated, bless even when cursed ...Jesus' ethic was expressly meant for this tough world, where good will and fair play from others are often not to be counted on, and where, if because of that, we justify our own ill will and inhumanity, there is no hope. For then mankind will go on, evil always met by evil, hatred met by hatred, violence arousing violence, injustice calling out injustice...
>
> Until mankind can do better than meet hate with hate, it heads for catastrophe.

I made the decision to follow Jesus, knowing that I would sometimes fall back into anger and self-pity, but knowing also that with the Lord's help I would be able to move out of that darkness. When some people continued to criticize me, especially a few who contended that I could not have loved my murdered children since I did not want their killer executed, I could only say, as the great Dutch philosopher Baruch Spinoza did, "Hatred can never do any good," and walk away.

Other information coming from the University of Michigan study interested me because it showed that women were more apt to forgive than were men and that older adults were much more likely to report they had forgiven people who had harmed them than were younger ones. That didn't surprise me, since time is said to heal many wounds, nor did another finding that those who forgave had better overall physical health than those who refused to forgive. Forgiveness frees the forgiver.

What Makes Forgiveness So Difficult

From the heartbreaking events in my life I feel I have learned much about what makes forgiveness so difficult and why it is so important to forgive. Holding onto anger and thoughts of wanting to "even the score" may make us feel stronger, perhaps a bit more powerful. But this is a fraud. The anger keeps us cemented to the one who harmed us. We give up freedom and the ability to get on with good work because we are tied to that phony but popular belief that we are justified in wanting to "get even."

So I learned that forgiveness begins with letting go of anger. Then, as freedom returns, we can find ourselves soaring again, no longer bogged down in our ego needs. Now we can go to the next stage of forgiveness, and that is to pray for the one who has hurt us—even the teenager who murdered our kids with a 9-millimeter gun—remembering that this person too is a child of God. The surprising development here is that the one forgiving is the one who reaps the benefits.

One might rightly ask, how can this be? I can answer from what I have learned: the fact is that if we don't forgive we end up internalizing what we hate, pushing God and love out of our souls. I saw this clearly in a movie released in early 1996 called *An Eye for an Eye*, starring Sally Field playing a mother whose daughter has been raped and murdered. The system fails by letting the murderer get off on a technicality. The mother then goes for revenge, buying a gun and learning to shoot so she can kill the man. Those responsible for this film had one thing in mind, to push the hate buttons in all of us, and it worked. At the end of the movie, when the mother pumped bullets into the rapist, everybody was hooting and hollering and clapping for the mother, who had now become a murderess herself.

I later saw Ms. Field on the *Oprah Winfrey Show* on television. The actress was asked if working on the film had led her to empathize with the mother. Ms. Field said no. The mother, she said, went down into herself and touched the dark places where latent evil dwells. She descended to become what the killer was. I admired Ms. Field for her insightful understanding of the evil of revenge. But

I don't think the movie audience got it. They had been force-fed the false power of "an eye for an eye," and they cheered for violence.

I have talked to many professionals in the field of psychology who say that persistent unforgiveness is part of human nature. But, pressed further, they also say that not forgiving someone who has betrayed you or deeply hurt you is devastatingly detrimental not only to your spiritual well-being but to your physical health as well. Even Confucius, China's most famous teacher/philosopher, spoke of the health problems brought on by unforgiveness. He said, chillingly, "If you devote your life to seeking revenge...dig two graves."

Choosing Forgiveness Over Revenge

Our late Pope John Paul II gave the world a profoundly moving lesson on the meaning of forgiveness when he visited Mehmet Ali Agca in Rome's Rebibbia prison just after Christmas in 1983. This was the man who had shot him thirty months earlier in St. Peter's Square. The pope went to the prison to present Agca with a silver rosary, and to give him a most important gift—his forgiveness.

At the time I spoke with many people who preferred revenge to forgiveness, who said, "Isn't it just weakness to forgive? Isn't that letting evildoers get away with their hurting actions?" I was glad to let Jesus, through the words of John Paul II, answer those questions. The pope stated, from his heart, "Forgiveness is above all a personal choice, a decision of the heart to go against the natural instinct to pay back evil with evil...Forgiveness may seem like weakness, but it demands great spiritual strength and moral courage, both in granting it and accepting it." Then our late pontiff added, "What sufferings are inflicted on humanity because of the failure to reconcile!"

After much prayer, and meeting with others who, like myself, had had to build a new life after suffering the torment of losing a loved one as a result of violence, I came to understand what makes forgiveness so difficult—in a word, anger. But I also began to see the light and the truth of what anger could do to me, keep me in a trap of hate. And that underscored the need to forgive.

A very special person I met was the Rev. Walter Everett, a Methodist minister who officiated at the wedding of Mike Carlucci—the murderer of his son. This man of God, who became my friend "Walt," bearing his intense pain, yet went to the prison to meet with his son's killer, believing that in some way this could help him find reconciliation and peace. "It blew me away," said Mike Carlucci when I met him some time later. "I had never had anyone forgive me in my life. I started crying. He said he wouldn't be able to live his life the way he lives it if he honestly didn't forgive me for this." Walt told me that forgiving Mike "doesn't remove the pain of Scott's death. But the additional pain of anger at Mike? I don't think I could have lived with that. By offering forgiveness, I freed myself from that hurt."

One of the most touching news stories I have ever read was that of the late Joseph Cardinal Bernadin of Chicago, in 1997, who forgave the man who had falsely accused him of sexual abuse years earlier. I can't imagine how devastatingly painful it must have been for the cardinal to have been so publicly humiliated by this vicious charge. Yet, what an

example he gave us when he sought a "meeting of reconciliation" to extend forgiveness to this troubled man, stating
that he bore no ill will toward him. Moreover, he taught us
that the pain he suffered not only contributed to his own
spiritual growth but also made him more compassionate.

When the story of Cardinal Bernadin's meeting with
his accuser Steven Cook, who later died of AIDS, was published, the cardinal's own words were, "May this story of
our meeting be a source of joy and grace to all who read it.
May God be praised." Certainly, this paralleled what Jesus
himself would have done and was a beautiful example of
forgiveness for all of us.

The Death Penalty Ignores Forgiveness

In the fall of 2005 I was invited by our Catholic bishops to
participate in the blessed work they called the "Catholic
Campaign to End the Use of the Death Penalty." They
asked me to join them because I had put forgiveness in action by working against the death penalty. At their meeting
in Washington, DC, Bishop Nicholas DiMarzio of
Brooklyn set the tone, asking: "What does the death
penalty do to us? What kind of society do we want to be?"
He noted that this is "not a liberal issue, but a life issue."
And, he added, "In the matter of life and death, no mistake
is acceptable. Death is irreversible."

Another person invited to participate in the effort was
someone named Kirk Bloodsworth, an innocent man who
might have been unjustly executed. He had been wrongly
convicted of the rape and murder of nine-year-old Dawn
Hamilton in 1984 and had spent nearly nine years on death

row before DNA proved him innocent. Kirk Bloodsworth, a Marine Corps veteran, continued to maintain his innocence, and among those who believed him was Deacon Al Rose, a Catholic prison chaplain who visited him in prison and taught him about the church. "The Catholic Church provided me with essential support in my time of need and I converted to Catholicism in 1989 while I was serving time behind bars," Kirk Bloodsworth told us.

His story was a striking example of the flaws in our criminal justice system, which was one of the problems addressed by the bishops. In a study of eighty-six criminal cases in which DNA evidence later exonerated the person convicted, it was found that there were forensic errors in 63 percent of these cases, and that in 19 percent of them, the defense attorney was incompetent. But the most common cause of erroneous conviction was eyewitness misidentification, and this is what happened in Mr. Bloodsworth's case.

To meet the soft-spoken and gentle Mr. Bloodsworth and his wife was truly a privilege for me. He expressed his sorrow to me that my son and his wife had been murdered, but also his respect that I could forgive the killer and would work to eliminate the death penalty anywhere this monstrous punishment is still in use.

When Kirk Bloodsworth was exonerated by DNA evidence, a fellow inmate named Kimberley Shay Ruffner, imprisoned for the attempted rape and stabbing of a Baltimore woman, congratulated him. Ten years later, Mr. Bloodsworth was told by Ann Brobst of the state's attorney's office that Ruffner had actually been the rapist and murderer of little Dawn Hamilton. Mr. Bloodsworth's first reaction was to shout at Ann Brobst, telling her that he had hated her for having called him a child killer and a monster. This was a very human reaction, and I think most people would have considered him justified in not forgiving those who had so unjustly condemned him. But then, remarkably, he followed up his angry words by stating, calmly and clearly, following the teaching of the Lord Jesus, "I forgive you."

Today, Mr. Bloodsworth works across America with the Justice Project on the need for prison reform. He has no hate for those responsible for his unjust conviction. "I forgive them all," he says. "God has to sort that out now."

Perhaps one of the most powerful examples of forgiveness in our time took place in the peaceful, God-loving Amish community of Nickel Mines, Pennsylvania. In early October 2006, a severely disturbed man entered a one-room schoolhouse where Amish children were respectfully and peacefully learning their lessons. His intent was to to sexually molest and kill the young girls there. After sending the boys and adults outside, he opened fire on a dozen girls and, after killing three of them, committed suicide. Two more children died of their wounds the following day.

News about this horrific crime immediately filled the nation's newspapers. Reporters and television interviewers kept referring to "revenge and hatred" for the killer, but when the Amish parents, relatives, and friends were asked to comment, they spoke of forgiveness. The headline in my in my daily paper read: "Amish Urge Forgiveness for Shooter." For many onlookers, this willingness to seek forgiveness rather than vengeance was astonishing. They simply could not understand it. Television reporters turned to professionals in mental health and religion to try to shed some light on how and why the Amish could be so forgiving.

One researcher, Gertrude Huntington, identified also as an "expert on children in Amish society," explained: "They know their children are going to heaven. They know their children are innocent...and they know they will join them in death." And then she added something that struck me deeply: "The hurt is very great, but they don't balance the hurt with hate."

The Recurring Question—Is Forgiveness Possible?

And yet, and yet...When you have been seared by horrible loss and pain, how can you fight the hate that overtakes you? I know what that feels like. I was thrown into that hell from the moment when I was informed that my son and daughter-in-law had been murdered. Then, in the space of one phone call, my entire life changed. I had to struggle with whether forgiveness was the right thing, whether it ever made sense, whether it was even possible.

I would break out in a sweat when I thought of the violence, the sin, that happened that night, when an eighteen-year-old named Joseph Shadow Clark slid through a basement window into their home, stealthily went up the stairs to the bedroom where they were sleeping, and shot them to death with his semi-automatic gun.

Every time I saw this in my mind's eye I shrank from the memory, paralyzed and powerless. I knew I had to reclaim my soul, but how? My children helped me as we struggled together, so damaged by this horror. We had always been opposed to the death penalty, and healing first began when we wrote to the judge, asking that Shadow Clark not be executed.

Then it was another mother, one who had moved beyond hatred and revenge after the murder of her daughter, who unknowingly helped me.

She began writing to the murderer, saying honestly, "This does not mean that I think you are innocent or that you are blameless for what happened." It was what she then said that made an imprint in my heart: "What I learned is this: You are a divine child of God. You carry the Christ-consciousness within you. You are surrounded by God's love even as you sit in your cell. *The Christ in me sends blessings to the Christ in you.*"

I cried my eyes out. Her words had helped me understand in a new way what Jesus meant by forgiveness, and why it must be a way of life, a way to live continuously. Now I could see that the minute we say "no" to forgiveness we are gouging Christ out of our life, and from that resulting emptiness of soul we have nothing left to give to anyone else.

This is what the Amish community knows and, from the midst of their tragedy, has shared with all of us.

Where All That Is Important Is Love

I heard an extraordinary story of forgiveness on public television in early 2007. It told of a remarkable woman named Immaculée Ilibagiza. She was a survivor of the 1994 genocide in Rwanda that pitted Hutus against Tutsis. Nearly one million people were slaughtered, including her parents and two brothers.

It was only because of the goodness of a local pastor that Immaculée and seven other Tutsi women escaped the machete-wielding killers looking for them. This good man hid the women in a tiny, dark bathroom where the seven of them huddled together, hardly able to move, for ninety-one days!

That Immaculée survived unbelievable horror is not why I still think of her. Not at all. It is what she has passed on to us that makes her stand out in my mind—and that is her love of God and her outspoken forgiveness for the killers of her family, friends, and neighbors

It wasn't until I read Immaculée's book, *Left to Tell*, written at the urging of noted spiritual speaker Wayne Dyer, that I really understood how she could forgive such evildoers. In her book Immaculée speaks often and profoundly of her Catholic faith, her love of the rosary, and how God helped her know she should open her heart to him so he could touch it with his infinite love.

She began to call that tight space in the bathroom her "sacred garden," where she spoke with God and meditated on his words. And the one word she heard over and over was "forgiveness." As she writes in her book, "I'd opened my heart to God and He'd touched it with His infinite love. For the first time, I pitied the killers. I asked God to forgive their sins and turn their souls toward His beautiful light."

But it was a dream she had that really solidified her faith. Jesus was standing in front of her, his arms outstretched, telling her that almost everyone she knew and loved had been killed. But then he told her, "They are with me now and they have joy. I will be your family." She awoke feeling that joy, assured that "God never breaks a promise."

Reading this, I remembered a dream from heaven that "saved me" after I had gotten the news of the murders of my son and his wife. John had entered my kitchen and came over to hug me. I called out joyfully to my other children, "John's here!" Then I asked, "John, why did you have to die?" for, while we knew who the killer was, we had no motive.

I kept repeating "Why?" and John started to go away. I begged him to come back, and then he did, to tell me not to question, but to forgive. "You see, Mom," he told me, "All that is important where I am is love."

No wonder I could relate so well to Immaculée!

When Immaculée and the women were finally able to leave their bathroom "cell," they saw the ruins of the village where they had lived and the corpses of the people they had known and loved. "We all shared in the misery that had descended upon the village, but I knew that the people gathered around me had lost much more than I had. They'd lost their faith—and in doing so, they'd also lost hope," she wrote.

Today, Immaculée, a woman of incredible strength, wisdom, and grace, works for the United Nations in New York. She is married to Byran Black, the Catholic man "sent by God to complete me," she writes. They have two children.

Forgiving: The Key to Freedom

As someone who had to confront the meaning and importance of forgiveness from my personal pain, I found a model in our late pope, John Paul II. I long saved a clipping of a lead story in the *New York Times* on April 14, 1997, with a headline that read, "Pope, in Sarajevo, Calls for Forgiveness." Once again, the pontiff was proclaiming one of the central teachings of Jesus, that we must forgive. And this day that key word was in big letters for all to see and think about—forgiveness.

The pope's words were powerful. "For the edifice of peace to be solid, against the background of so much blood and hatred, it will have to build on the courage of forgiveness." Reading those words, I prayed intensely that the world would take notice, listen, and find the courage Pope John Paul II was talking about. Because it does take courage. To forgive takes an indescribable strength.

By a strange coincidence, I had heard that message in person only the night before, when St. Joseph's Church in Brookfield, Connecticut, had hosted a talk by Officer Stephen McDonald, a brave man with an incredible story. I have twice been privileged to work with him. Eleven years ago, while working as a New York City police officer, he had been shot in Central Park by a teenager. The wound had left him paralyzed, unable to move his arms or legs. Remarkably, Stephen McDonald had refused to stop living. He found himself in a new "mission"—that of being a living witness to the beauty of life and the power of forgiveness to help you live that life for God and others.

Officer McDonald said he chose to forgive the fifteen-year-old who shot him (and who sadly was killed in a motorcycle accident two weeks after having served eight years in prison) because he wanted to move on and to help others. He would have been stuck in his anger, bitter and without peace, had he not forgiven Shavod Jones.

Some 150 people came to hear Officer Stephen McDonald, a man who was determined, in spite of his disabling injuries, to make his life meaningful and share his message of faith and forgiveness with others. About a third of those who came were young people, because the sponsors of this talk were, admirably, St. Joseph's youth group. Officer McDonald spoke of his reliance on the Mass, the Eucharist, the rosary—and his family—for the renewal of his spirituality. The enthusiastic response of the young people there for his talk was heartwarming.

I think I was meant to be focusing on forgiveness that week, because the same day on which I went to hear Officer McDonald, I had just finished reading a manuscript by Johann Christoph Arnold, of the Bruderhof Community, entitled *Seventy Times Seven: The Power of Forgiveness.*

In his manuscript Pastor Arnold—known in Catholic circles for his powerful book, *A Plea for Purity*—told more than twenty-five stories of people who found a life after gaining the courage to forgive. These are stories of people who had suffered in the Holocaust, from interracial prejudice, from infidelity in marriage, people who had lost children, homes, positions. I was very moved by the truth that emerged from the stories—that it is out of suffering that we humans come to learn the power and truth of Jesus' words about the necessity for forgiveness.

"Instead of leaving us weak and vulnerable, forgiving strengthens and empowers our lives and our work," Pastor Arnold wrote. "More than that, it sets into motion a positive chain-reaction, which brings the fruits of our forgiveness to others. We see our own need for forgiveness; we realize the extent of God's love to us and must pour out that love to all."

Stephen McDonald's message is the same. He says he's "closer to heaven now," and so can even thank God for his injuries. We all have much to learn from people who have suffered and still forgive.

Again, I repeat, forgiving doesn't mean giving in, it means letting go, and letting go is a pre-condition to becoming free. If you don't forgive, you hand over to the one who hurt you ever more control over you. Had I not forgiven Shadow Clark, I would be emotionally handcuffed to him, bound to him in a destructive way. Jesus said that he came "to set us free," and he showed us the way. That way was, in a word, forgiveness. It was a contradictory path for his times, and it remains a contradictory path in our time.

Forgiveness is an attribute of the strong. The weak can never forgive.

—Mohandas Gandhi

6
GOD'S NON-NEGOTIABLE RULE FOR HUMAN INTERACTION

The forgiveness of enemies is based upon a profound spiritual response in the face of unjust suffering, a response formed in the soul's experience of how God himself compassionately holds and loves the world... The prayer for the forgiveness of enemies represents the triumph of divine grace working in and through human nature, fashioning the soul so that it feels towards the world as God himself does.

—*William Reiser, SJ*

I shall long remember being verbally accosted by an angry woman when, as a mother of murder victims, I was giving a talk on "The Why of Forgiveness." She had done her Bible homework, she said, and could prove that vindictiveness and vengeance were based on God's law. She quoted first Psalm 109, "a prayer for vindication and vengeance," and then the New Testament, speaking Jesus' words, "For all who take to the sword shall perish by the sword." She interpreted this to mean that all killers should be not forgiven, but killed.

Then, shaking her head, she told me that my "wrong notion" of forgiveness was a "Johnny-come-lately" thing, put together by "liberals and idealists, like you." I was shaking my head, too, for there is nothing "Johnny-come-lately" about forgiveness. I reminded her of the very early Old Testament story of the murder of Abel by his brother Cain. God "marks" Cain on his forehead precisely so that he may be protected from being killed. God is very clear about this, and he says, "Whoever kills Cain will suffer a sevenfold vengeance."

In this scene, God was clearly not in favor of capital punishment, of human beings imposing the death penalty. In fact, God's words indicate that our creator wanted to stop, then and there, any possible cycle of violence emerging in his newly created world. He showed early on that he is a forgiving God. After I said this, the woman walked away from me, still shaking her head.

Admittedly, forgiveness is not easy, yet if we believe the teachings of the Lord Jesus, who can deny that forgiveness is the crucial key that opens the door to heaven for us? Why else would Jesus have given us his prayer with the astounding petition to his Father—to forgive us our sins *as we forgive* those who sin against us?

As for how necessary it was for Jesus to underscore the essential role of forgiveness in gaining salvation, we have only to look back in time and see how people have treated one another since the dawn of human history. Long before the time of Jesus, the world had to deal with evils of all kinds, from individual crimes of person against person to the hostilities generated by those wanting to seize power over others by waging violence and war.

Yet even in ancient times, there were some wise people who understood there to be a divine rule for how human beings should relate to one another. More than three millennia ago the call for forgiveness rang out in the Rig Veda, the Hindu scriptures: "God will forgive the sinner if he earnestly casts away his sin. Human forgiveness is the way to happiness among men. A wise man will always be ready to forgive."

In the sixth century BCE, an ancient Chinese sage named Laotzu believed and wrote that we are all "members of one another." Laotzu is credited with having written a book called the *Tao Te Ching*. Witter Bynner, one of the numerous translators of this book, referred to Laotzu and Jesus as "ethical fellows." In writing about the devastation of war, which in obvious and understandable ways blocks forgiveness, Laotzu said:

> Even the finest arms are an instrument of evil,
> A spread of plague,
> And the way for a vital man to go is not the way of
>   a soldier.
> But in time of war men civilized in peace
> Turn from their higher to their lower nature.
> Arms are an instrument of evil,
> No measure for thoughtful men
> Until there fail all other choice
> But sad acceptance of it.
> Triumph is not beautiful.
> He who thinks triumph beautiful
> Is one with a will to kill,

And one with a will to kill
Shall never prevail upon the world.
It is a good sign when man's higher nature comes
    forward,
A bad sign when his lower nature comes forward,
When retainers take charge
And the master stays back
As in the conduct of a funeral.
The death of a multitude is cause for mourning:
Conduct your triumph as a funeral.

Yet to this day, wars go on, killing abounds, and hatreds fester, even while voices of wisdom still call for forgiveness. Four hundred years before the time of Jesus, Buddha's voice was another of these voices. Like Jesus, he too pointed out the importance of forgiveness: "Hatreds do not ever cease in this world by hating, but by love; this is an eternal truth...Overcome anger by love, overcome evil by good. Overcome the miser by giving; overcome the liar by truth...This is the ancient and eternal law."

Centuries later, another wise man, named Marcus Aurelius Antoninus, made his mark on the world by becoming emperor of Rome in the year 161 CE. Students of history who have read his *Meditations* are often inspired by his literary gifts and the keen sense of morality that is evident in his writings. In translations by scholar George Long, we meet a man who

constantly recurs to his fundamental principle that
the universe is wisely ordered, that every man is a
part of it and must conform to that order which he

cannot change, that whatever the Deity has done is good, and that all mankind are a man's brethren, that he must love and cherish them better, even those who would do him harm...

Antoninus teaches in various passages the forgiveness of injuries, and we know he also practiced what he taught...Antoninus often enforces it and gives us aid towards following it. When we are injured, we feel anger and resentment, and the feeling is natural, just and useful for the conservation of society. It is useful that wrong-doers should feel the natural consequences of their actions...But revenge, in the proper sense of that word, must not be practiced. "The best way of avenging thyself," says the emperor, "is not to become like the wrongdoer."

According to George Long, the Roman leader believes that "a man must not retire into solitude and cut himself off from his fellow men...All men are his kin, not only in blood, but still more by participating in the same intelligence and by being a portion of the same divinity." In his writings the emperor states, "Love mankind. Follow God..."

Remarkably—and sadly—in the reign of an emperor who had such a noble soul and so much wisdom, constant warfare erupted on the frontiers of the Roman empire, forcing him to command armies that suffered tremendous reversals. Worse, a severe pestilence erupted, throwing his people into a panic. Believing they were suffering from the anger of the gods, they needed to find a scapegoat, and so they placed the blame on the Christians. Historians report that the emperor Antoninus sanctioned a cruel persecution of the Christians, a stain on his record. According to his biographer Professor Long, however, "we cannot admit that such a man was an active persecutor, for there is no evidence that he was, though it is certain that he had no good opinion of the Christians."

If the emperor Antoninus needed forgiveness for his actions against Christians, Catholics were reminded, back in the "jubilee" year of 2000, that our church, too, needed to seek forgiveness for some of the wrongs it had done in the past. At that time, the president of the International Theological Commission, Joseph Cardinal Ratzinger—now our Pope Benedict XVI—in conjunction with Pope John Paul II, proposed a study on the topic "Memory and Reconciliation: The Church and the Faults of the Past."

Traditionally, a jubilee year was proclaimed as a time to make a fresh start, to throw off those chains that block one from God, to become free. It became a time of forgiveness for people carrying debts and burdens, resentments and hatreds. In a jubilee year, the church offered an invitation to all to come, to ask for healing, and to be made whole and joyful.

A picture that will always remain framed in my memory is that of our late Pope John Paul II, kneeling before the cross at St. Peter's Basilica in Rome, and his words in the ceremony of apology:

> Before Christ, who for love bore our sins, we are all invited to a deep examination of conscience. One of the characteristic elements of the great jubilee lies in what I have described as *purification of memory*. I ask that in this year of mercy, the church, strengthened by the holiness that she receives from her Lord, kneel before God and beg for forgiveness for past and present sins of her sons. *We forgive and we ask forgiveness.*

In the papal document formally convoking the jubilee year, Pope John Paul II explained his insistence on "purification of memory" to be "an act of courage and humility in recognizing the wrongs done by those who have borne the name of Christian."

The International Theological Commission document, "Memory and Reconciliation," acknowledged that

> Indeed, in the entire history of the Church there are no precedents for requests for forgiveness by the Magisterium for past wrongs. Councils and papal decrees applied sanctions, to be sure, to abuses of which clerics and laymen were found guilty, and many pastors sincerely strove to correct them. However, the occasions when ecclesiastical authorities—Popes, Bishops, Councils—have openly acknowledged the faults or abuses which they themselves were guilty of, have been quite rare.

The document noted that Pope John Paul II also "extended a request for forgiveness to a multitude of historical events in which the Church, or individual groups of Christians, were implicated in different respects." Nor did he ignore "historical phenomena like the Crusades or the Inquisition," or leave out "the situations of 'social sin'— which are evident in the human community when justice, freedom and peace are damaged..."

Especially and always to be underscored, the document points out, are the commands by Jesus in the New Testament. Most important of all is "love for one's neighbor." Absolutely central in the teaching of Jesus, this becomes the new commandment in the Gospel of John: "The Christian is called to love and to forgive to a degree that transcends every human standard of justice and produces a reciprocity between human beings, reflective of the reciprocity between Christ and the Father. In this perspective, great emphasis is given to the theme of reconciliation and forgiveness of faults."

Not forgotten in the document is the "tormented history" of the relations between Christians and Jews.

The Shoah was certainly the result of the pagan ideology that was Nazism, animated by a merciless anti-Semitism that not only despised the faith of the Jewish people, but also denied their very human dignity. Nevertheless, it may be asked whether the Nazi persecution of the Jews was not made easier by the anti-Jewish prejudices imbedded in some Christian minds and hearts...

Did Christians give every possible assistance to those being persecuted, and in particular to the persecuted Jews? There is no doubt that there were many Christians who risked their lives to save and to help their Jewish neighbors. It seems, however, also true, that alongside such courageous men and women, the spiritual resistance and concrete action of other Christians was not that which might have been expected from Christ's followers...The hostility or mistrust shown by numerous Christians towards Jews over the course of time is a painful historical fact...which requires repentance...

The Importance of Reconciliation

The Vatican document underscored a word that definitely needed a revival in the church: *reconciliation*. Not an easy subject to talk about, and perhaps the most misunderstood word in Christian teaching, it is just about the most important mandate in our Christian faith.

Reconciliation has to do with removing the obstacles that lie in the way of our intimate union with God and with our fellow men and women. In his parables, in his healings, in his life, death, and resurrection, Jesus continually preached the essential importance of reconciliation. The life of a disciple of Jesus is essentially a life of reconciliation, because this is how God wants his people to relate to one another.

In practice, reconciliation means coming together as a family—God's family—holding no grudges, no anger, no meanness, and doing no harm to one another. It requires forgiveness—the word that Jesus spoke over and over.

Forgiveness is the blueprint for reconciliation with God, with others, with the world, and even with oneself. Whenever we come together to participate in the sacrament of reconciliation, celebrating the sacrament of penance, we are giving witness to something astonishing— our true identity as the body of Christ.

If we look into church history, going back to about the year 150, we find the beginnings of a ritual for forgiveness —but the rite was a very public one. It was communal. The sinner would come forward and ask forgiveness, yet reconciliation required that the Christian community pray for the sinner.

Over the next several hundred years, the public ritual of reconciliation was modified and underwent a name change. The Celtic monks had a lot to do with this. They altered the Roman form of forgiveness, which was public, and initiated a form of penance that was private. The focus then shifted from community well-being and solidarity with the community to the individual's private experience of forgiveness and healing and consolation. The operative word became "confession"—not "reconciliation."

By the thirteenth century church leaders were actively promoting this private form of confession and the term "reconciliation" was hardly heard again until the twentieth century. Theologians then began to study the sacrament of penance in depth and rediscovered reconciliation as it was practiced in the early centuries of the church.

By the time Pope John XXIII convoked the Second Vatican Council, some theologians were calling for a pastoral renewal of the sacrament of penance. Vatican II then changed the ritual so that it would once again reflect the fact that sin has a communal dimension, that sin is basically an offense against both God and the community. To fix the brokenness that results from sin, we have to get together. We can't do it alone. It is the job of the whole community. And so this means we cannot claim to be people of faith, cannot bring our gift to the altar of God, without first undergoing the cleansing that requires that we be reconciled with our neighbors. Jesus put it quite clearly: "When you are offering your gift at the altar, if you remember that your brother or sister has something against you, leave your gift there before the altar and go: first be reconciled with your brother or sister, and the come and offer your gift" (Mt 5:23).

That's what reconciliation is all about—us, our neighbors, and God—relating to one another as God wants. Getting to that place is hinged—absolutely—on forgiveness.

In the spirit of that great jubilee year of 2000, a remarkable action took place in the Diocese of Rockville Center in Long Island, New York, during Holy Week. Priests of all the 134 parishes were asked to be available for the sacrament of reconciliation from 4 PM to 10 PM on a specific day so that everyone could have the opportunity to celebrate this sacrament. For many, that sounded strange, especially considering the declining numbers of Catholics going to confession in recent years.

The diocese did a publicity blitz, on radio and in newspapers, emphasizing that the sacrament was not about condemnation but about reconciliation. A handbook made available to all emphasized that to examine one's conscience did not mean coming up with "a grocery list of sins," but rather was to be "a reflection on the rhythms of one's daily life and the relationship that person has with himself, with others and with God."

The diocese offered this invitation, and it was a gamble. No one could have predicted how it would turn out. In the weeks before this unusual day, the *Long Island Catholic*, the diocesan paper, had invited people to send in their comments about confession. The majority response was negative, with comments like, "I never received advice or consolation in confession—just a feeling of being very uncomfortable." Another wrote, "I feel confession is a waste of time and I get nothing out of it." And the saddest was, "I am gay. Every time I went to confession I was made to feel like some subhuman form of life. No priest ever told me

God loves me as I am. The last time was 1977. I have been celibate for almost 20 years... I go to church every week ... the Church just doesn't want us. People keep telling me confession is different today and I should go, but I can't bring myself to do it."

Still, the diocese made every effort to get the word out that this day would have nothing to do with punishment or embarrassment. "Don't worry about what to do when you get there. Just get there. The sacrament is not about judgment, let alone condemnation. It's about forgiveness," was the constantly reiterated message.

When the day finally arrived, all the parishes reported that streams of people showed up, hundreds of them responding to this first-time-ever massive invitation. A priest I spoke to said that the turnout was absolutely remarkable, that people had long hungered for such a call, anxious and ready to free themselves of what had kept them from God, some because of mere indifference, some for past serious sins.

I was impressed with the beautiful words of one of the diocese's pastors, Msgr. Frank Gaeta, who, speaking of reconciliation, said the challenge of the church is to get away from legalism and go to the heart and mind of Jesus. The church's life, Msgr. Gaeta points out, is all about "table fellowship," about sharing together in God's house, a place where everybody is welcome.

Forgiveness Is an Act of Grace

Forgiveness is strongly linked to God, because forgiveness is, indisputably, an act of grace. If we think back to the stories we have heard that have to do with good and evil, grace—received or destroyed—is always the centerpiece. This is most vividly evident in stories told through the medium of film.

One of the finest movies I have ever seen is *Amazing Grace*, the story of William Wilberforce, an Englishman who was born into a well-to-do family of British merchants and who, because of God's grace, became a leading advocate of social reform. He had been elected to Parliament at the age of twenty-one, but soon found what he believed was his true calling when he became an Evangelical Christian. The resulting major changes in his lifestyle included his involvement with and eventual leadership in the abolitionist movement, which sought to put an end to the slave trade. This horrific practice involved abducting black men and women from their African homes and putting them on ships to the West Indies where they were sold as slaves. The conditions were so terrible that scores of these people died. Some honest people called the slave trade "commercial war."

While the selling enriched many white people, "in the record of the journey from Africa to the West are the endless tales of whole cargoes of captives leaping overboard into the ocean, throwing their infants overboard; mass suicides, mutinies, fasting to death. They were beaten, killed and destroyed by plague—but always some survived," wrote Earl Conrad, a crusader against racial prejudice, in his 1966 book, *The Invention of the Negro*.

One of the people who strongly influenced William Wilberforce was John Newton, a former slave ship captain who had had a dramatic religious conversion and had experienced extreme remorse. He believed that it was the grace of God that had brought him to see the evil of what he was doing and that, in asking for forgiveness, he would receive it. So moved was he by this revelation that he wrote the hymn "Amazing Grace."

William Wilberforce, deeply influenced by John Newton and his hymn, worked tirelessly against slavery for the next twenty years. His work, along with that of others who had come to see the sinfulness of the slave trade and the need to seek forgiveness by ending this "commerce," was finally successful. Great Britain ended its role in the slave trade on March 25, 1807.

The movie about William Wilberforce was, as its title signifies, a story about grace. Another movie, called *The Mission*, deals only peripherally with the slave trade, but it includes a powerful scene that wordlessly and graphically sums up what the grace of forgiveness means. In this film a slave trader, played by Robert De Niro, finds an unusual way to escape prison for the killing of his own brother. He joins some Jesuit monks traveling to work at a mission in Latin America. In a strange form of self-imposed repentance, he embarks on this difficult journey through jungles and over mountains carrying a bagful of heavy weapons.

Finally, they all reach the top of the last mountain, and the slave trader suddenly comes face-to-face with a child who is holding a huge knife in his hand. The boy is the son of one of the natives the trader had captured and dragged away from his people to be sold as a slave.

At that moment, it would seem the child would be justified in using the knife to get revenge for the loss of his father. But he doesn't kill the trader. He uses the knife to cut the ropes of the bag burdening the man. The weapons go tumbling down the side of the mountain.

The boy's act of forgiveness is so startling, so Jesus-like, that the slave trader is literally catapulted into the arms of God. He has been the recipient of a grace that will change his life.

I saw this movie as I was reading the works of philosopher William James, who, writing of the saints, said they "...may, with their extravagances of human tenderness, be prophetic...Treating those whom they met, in spite of the past, in spite of all appearances, as worthy, they have stimulated them to *be* worthy, miraculously transformed them by their radiant example..."

The saints were the people who lived in such a way of goodness that God could look on them and say of them— as he says now and will say in ages to come of all who live in the same way of goodness—"This one takes after me."

Jesus was One who showed by word and by work, by trial and by triumph, by smiting and by smile, by goodness and by service what the Heart of the universe is like...We know now what God's life is and what man's life ought to be—Christlike.

—E. Stanley Jones

7
FORGIVENESS—
ALWAYS PRESENT TENSE

When Christ confronts those who contributed to his death, he speaks words, not of retribution, but of reconciliation and compassion. Mind you, the awful texture of the disorder is not for a moment overlooked—that is the integrity of the judgment—but the problem is resolved through nonviolence and forgiveness.

—*Robert Barron*

There was a time when the only way most people had of learning about "man's inhumanity to man" was by reading about it in newspapers or magazines or hearing about it on the radio. Then came moving pictures and newsreels, and we could see it all on a big screen in a theater. Now, of course, with television and the Internet, we no longer have to leave home to be exposed to all the ways people have of hurting one another. As I write this, I have just finished viewing a troubling news report of teen girls badly beating another girl, chosen as their victim for a titillating "show" they were planning to put on the Internet.

This kind of behavior is beyond appalling. No wonder people have a problem with the command Jesus gave us to forgive. But Jesus was dealing with reality. Knowing that his coming would not eliminate sin, he gave us a way to conquer it, and that way was forgiveness.

I would wager that everyone has a family story about forgiveness or the lack of it. I remember one such story told to me a long time ago by a woman I worked with at one of my summer jobs as a teenager. She had a younger sister, she said, who had lied about her to their father, accusing her of having sneaked out of the house one night to meet her boyfriend. Their father, an immigrant from Italy who strictly controlled his daughters' activities, was so angry that he made her move out and live with her aunt, his mean sister. Understandably, this was a traumatic experience for her, but she told me that it had all happened a long time ago. Now she was married and had two children. Knowing that I went to daily Mass, she would often tell me what a devout Catholic she was, adding that she never missed Mass on Sundays.

One day I happened to ask her if she now had a good relationship with her sister. "I forgave her, and that was enough," she answered coldly. She no longer saw her sister or even talked to her. Although I was only a teenager, I could sense that she was still carrying her anger. It was evident in the very tone of her voice. Even back then I was already beginning to understand that to say "I forgave" didn't work, that there is no such thing as a past tense for forgiveness. As the decades went by and I had to deal with many deep hurts, I came to understand that Jesus' commandment is always present tense—or it's a sham.

Perhaps because forgiveness has been a major part of my own life, I have looked for support from many reconciliation accounts, past and present, and often have found them in unexpected places. Some time ago I was deeply moved by a story that appeared on the front page of my local daily newspaper. The headline was "Mystery Chairloom," and the subtitle read, "Family Keepsake Hid Secret Message."

The newspaper article told of a chair that had recently been brought by two sisters to an upholsterer. When the man took the old seat out, he discovered a series of dots, like dominos, burned into the rail that had been hidden behind the chair's seat. Clearly, it looked like a message, but what did it mean?

When the sisters, Nancy Kear-Johnson and Kathi Kear Rainville, were interviewed for the article, they said that the chair had been given to their great grand-uncle, New York Judge Edward B. Kear, by an inmate at Sing Sing, the notorious prison in New York State, a century ago. The prisoner had made the beautifully carved, upholstered chair as a thank-you gift for this judge, even though he was the man who had sent him to prison. Passed down through four generations in the family was a story saying that somewhere in the chair was a hidden message from the prisoner to the judge. Now, for the first time, with the appearance of the dots, the story appeared to be true.

The newspaper article included a picture of the chair rail and ended by asking any reader who could crack the code and decipher the message to come forward.

As I read the story, what really caught my attention was what the sisters said about their relative, a Republican judge in Westchester County, New York, in the late 1800s. He had been a Quaker, and—almost unheard of for an important person of the courts—he would stay in touch with the men he had sentenced, visiting many of them while they were in prison. Apparently he visited this one man at Sing Sing on a regular basis and helped him change his life for the better. In gratitude, the man had made the chair and given it to the judge as a gift. From the time of his release from prison until his death in 1911 the man stayed in touch with the judge.

I have done a great deal of prison work since my son and his wife were murdered, and the impersonalism and utter disregard for rehabilitation of inmates that I see in our criminal justice system today is a far cry from the human concern I read about in that story. If prisoners today could be visited by the judges who sentenced them, judges willing to express concern and compassion, as Judge Kear did, my guess is that we would see a significant reduction in the high recidivism rate. There would be far fewer cases of released prisoners, made worse by their experience behind bars, returning to crime.

There's a wonderful postscript to this mystery story. The riddle of the dots was decoded by an area woman named Phaedre Fayad. The prisoner's message was "*I am innocent, but I forgive thee.*" It's worth noting that that the prisoner didn't say, "I forgave." He said, "I forgive." There is no question in my mind that this prisoner fully understood what he was saying. He knew that there was no way to "forgive and forget," no way to put all his pain in the past tense. He had to forgive continually. It would always be present tense.

Today we have two million-plus inmates in our nation's prisons. We're finding an uncomfortable number to be innocent, many because of DNA testing. Still others claim they are innocent, but because of legal glitches, or because they have no money for lawyers, they are unable to have their cases tried again, and so they remain in prison. If they had a Judge Kear in their lives, perhaps they, too, could be moved to forgive.

There is another prisoner forgiveness story, this one from British history, that long ago caught my attention. It was an account of the execution of Mary Stuart, a Catholic and queen of Scotland, during the reign of Queen Elizabeth I in the sixteenth century. The account was written by John Lingard, a celebrated British historian who was also a Catholic priest. Why Mary was taken from her country, arrested, imprisoned in the notorious Tower of London, seen as a threat by Queen Elizabeth, and ultimately brought to the execution site and beheaded still challenges many historians.

What is known is that Elizabeth, who was Protestant, felt that so long as the Catholic Mary lived, she would pose a dangerous threat to her own position. In spite of the fact that Mary was the sovereign queen of another country, Elizabeth had her tried by an English court and condemned. After being confined in the Tower of London for eighteen years, Mary was put to death. During the years of her imprisonment and until the very end of Mary's life, as she was being taken to the place of execution, Queen Elizabeth tried to get her to renounce the Catholic Church.

Instead, as Fr. Lingard writes, Mary "thanked her God that he had given her this opportunity of publicly professing her religion...*she pardoned from her heart all her enemies...*"

Historians say the execution scene was chilling, yet marked by the great sense of personal dignity with which Mary met her fate, still forgiving those who had condemned her. When the time came for her to walk to the scaffold, she held up the crucifix she carried and exclaimed, "As thy arms, O God, were stretched out upon the cross, so receive me into the arms of thy mercy and forgive me my sins." Thanks to a little known historian in a Roman collar, Mary, who was forty-four years old when she died in 1587, is remembered by us today as the murdered queen who was forgiving.

We can look at any period of history and find events involving actions by governments, groups, and individuals that have left victims dead, or mourning, or raging for revenge. Not a week goes by that I do not hear a reference to 9/11, too often couched in words tinged by long-held anger. The tragedy of September 11, 2001, has been described over and over as an act of aggression that forced our nation into war. The enemy was never specific. It was a "war on terrorism," and the enemy was faceless.

This amorphous definition instilled fear in the hearts of Americans, a fear that was fostered and fed by a small but powerful group of policy makers in the White House who wanted to move ahead with a long-planned change for America. We would now put our potential action as the

world's "superpower" on the front burner, permitting ourselves to throw our weight around, launching "preemptive
military strikes," and making up new rules as we went
along.

For Some People Revenge Is Not the Way

Although I have heard many say that we don't "forgive" enemies, that we get "revenge," and that we now have a "right"
to declare wars wherever we feel "terrorists" may be har-
bored, some very special individuals feel differently. They
are relatives of people who were killed in the September 11
massacre, and they have no interest in vengeance. There are
nearly one hundred of them, and they have set up an organization they call "Families for Peaceful Tomorrows."

Colleen Kelly, whose brother was killed, explains what
they're about. "We don't want violence perpetuated as a
way to retaliate or avenge their deaths. If we're ever going
to heal, we have to be able to say, even though great injustices have occurred against us, 'I forgive you.'"

According to its "mission statement," the organization
was formed "to seek effective non-violent responses to terrorism, and identify a commonality with all people simi-
larly affected by violence throughout the world. By consci-
entiously exploring peaceful options in our search for
justice, we choose to spare additional innocent families the
suffering that we have already experienced as well as to
break the endless cycle of violence and retaliation engen-
dered by war."

The group chose its name from a quote by Martin
Luther King: "War makes poor chisels for carving out

peaceful tomorrows." "That's what we're all about," says Colleen. "We don't want 9/11 used for more violence."

This young Catholic mother of three traveled to Iraq to "see the faces of the Iraqi people...It makes it harder to wage a war when you humanize the people. You have to ask, how do we see Christ and ourselves in the other?"

Colleen commended the U.S. Catholic Conference of Bishops "for their moral leadership in opposing the Iraq war. I'm pretty sure Jesus would not advocate the bombing of any country," she said, adding that "for self-preservation, we have to find other ways," the most important and effective of which is forgiveness.

Some of the most powerful stories of forgiveness have to do with the Holocaust, the Nazi attempt to annihilate the Jewish people. I have read so many books on this terrible tragedy, and I still am amazed at how it was possible for so many survivors to speak not of hatred, but of forgiveness. Only recently a friend sent me a story written by Jason Song, a *Los Angeles Times* staff writer, titled "Her Holocaust Pardon Inspires Others."

The article was about a talk given by Eva Kor, a Holocaust survivor, to a Jewish congregation in California. In her presentation Eva described how she was taken to Auschwitz in 1944 when she was ten years old, along with her parents and three siblings. After arriving in Auschwitz, Eva and her twin sister Miriam were separated from the others and taken to the facility where the infamous Dr. Josef Mengele was conducting experiments on twins. She and her sister managed to survive, and after the Allies liberated the camp, she traveled to Israel, eventually married another Holocaust survivor, and then moved to Terre Haute, Indiana.

Surprisingly, she one day received a letter from another of the Nazi doctors, Dr. Hans Munch, asking her and other survivors of Auschwitz for forgiveness. When she responded by expressing her forgiveness of all the Nazis who had worked on Dr. Mengele's experiments, she "immediately felt a burden of pain lift," she told the audience, adding that she has since "tried to promote the power of forgiveness."

Even more impressive was the conclusion of this story, when an audience member, eighty-five-year-old Sidi Grunstein Gluck, told of how she and her brother were the only ones in their family to have survived the Holocaust. As Jason Song writes,

> But after being freed from a camp, Gluck passed a train full of hungry German soldiers. She reached into her pocket and gave the men a piece of bread. "That's the way my mother raised me. If someone is hungry, you give them something to eat," said Gluck.

That is, indeed, forgiveness, present tense!

I think that stories of forgiveness can help us remain firm in our commitment to this most important of teachings given to us by Jesus. In course of my own life I have found that the "discovery" of such stories has come when I most needed reaffirmation of the importance of constantly renewing forgiveness. Most recently, thanks to the great composer Mozart, I have discovered yet another story about this.

I had been reading about this wonderful composer, taking note of what the late tenor Luciano Pavarotti had said of him: "I don't think Mozart was a composer; he was a carrier, a messenger from God, sent here with the music already written." Curious about this, I went back to a music book I have had for over sixty years, written by Sigmund Spaeth, whose voice I had heard explaining Metropolitan Opera performances every Saturday on the radio when I was a teenager. Professor Spaeth writes that Mozart had had "a premonition of death" and then goes on to explain:

> There is a knock on the door, and a stranger enters. He is dressed in gray, coldly somber and forbidding in appearance. He hands Mozart a letter and vanishes. It is an order for a *Requiem Mass*, but from whom it comes is a mystery. The composer may name his own price, but the identity of his patron must remain a secret. Mozart...cannot escape a strange feeling that it is Death himself who has commanded this final work from his inspired pen.

Mozart begins to compose this Requiem immediately, but is unexpectedly asked to write an opera to celebrate the crowning of Emperor Leopold II as King of Bohemia. He is handed a libretto, titled *La Clemenza di Tito*.

I had never heard of this opera until after my son John and his wife Nancy were murdered, and we, as a family, asked the judge not to impose the death penalty on their killer. My son Paul and my daughter Mary were among many New Yorkers who were supporting a resolution to pass a moratorium on executions in New York State. Tears filled my eyes when I heard Mary, then studying opera, say: "Perhaps it was no coincidence that I was singing *La Clemenza di Tito* the night I heard of John and Nancy's murder. For in that opera composed by Mozart over two hundred years ago in 1791, the Emperor Titus struggles mightily over whether or not to impose the death penalty..."

What has happened is that the emperor has been betrayed by his two best friends. Locked in a struggle within himself, he feels he could never forgive his friends, and so, in agony, he signs a death warrant.

Mary goes on: "He is torn between his personal anger and his enlightened mind. His passion wants revenge while his wisdom tells him there is a better, more reasoned way to live. In the end, Titus decides to choose clemency. Two hundred years after Mozart, we can do just as well."

I have since wondered if Mozart accepted the commission to write this opera about forgiveness because of the strange man who appeared with the request and money to have a Requiem written. Mozart was not in good health at this time. Perhaps he did indeed have a premonition of death and consequently saw the need to forgive the many people who had made his life and work at times cruelly difficult.

Strangely enough, as I was writing this book on forgiveness, I noticed that the Metropolitan Opera was putting on a production of *La Clemenza di Tito*. I was struck by the coincidence, and couldn't help but wonder if it might be a sign for me, personally, for I had been newly struggling with forgiveness for the killer of my son and daughter-in-law. As a family we had long-ago offered our forgiveness to this young man, Joseph Shadow Clark, and he responded, to my surprise, twelve years later, in May, 2005, with a brief letter:

> Dear Antoinette Bosco and Family:
> I am very sorry for what I did. Please forgive me. I am extremely sorry for the pain I have caused you and your family. Please accept my humble apology, and if you can find it within your heart, please forgive me.
>
> Humbly,
> Joseph Shadow Clark

I responded right away, telling him that my children and I were "deeply moved" by his letter, and adding,

> We have always been forgiving people and have extended our forgiveness to you in all these years. That's not to say we can understand what you did. Nor do we think you should be out of prison. We must always be accountable for our actions, especially when they cause permanent hurt to others.
> My life changed quite radically after the murders. I had to leave my job as an editor of a newspaper, and I started writing books that dealt with how to "find peace from pain," and how to keep believing in God when your faith gets shattered. But I had always been a person of great faith in the

goodness of the Lord. And I had always believed in the teachings of Jesus, who told us to love, to be merciful, to forgive, to feed the hungry, to visit the prisoners. So I prayed endlessly for Him to help me to forgive, and I was helped in this by going into a difficult "ministry," visiting and working with prisoners.

You may not believe this, but I have prayed for you ever since I was told that you were "the shooter." My children and I asked so many times, "What turns an 18-year old into a killer?" Since I felt I would never have an answer, all I could do was pray for you, asking God to help you seek forgiveness. When your letter came, I cried, thanking God that you had asked for forgiveness.

My children and I have also been always opposed to the death penalty, and we were saddened that Montana had reestablished that horror. Fearful that you might face that ultimate punishment, we wrote to the judge asking him to spare you from a death sentence. We were very relieved when you took a plea bargain, so you would have the chance to repent for your crime, perhaps continue your education, and still do good with your young life.

I hope you will write to me, telling me of your situation in prison, what kind of work or education is available to you. Do you still practice your Christian faith?

...I hope you and your family have a joyful Easter season.

In my letter to him I also mentioned that I had written a book called *Choosing Mercy: Mother of Murder Victims Pleads to End the Death Penalty*, and I asked him if he would be interested in receiving a copy of it. When he wrote back, he said "Your forgiveness and prayers mean a lot to me," and added that yes, he did want a copy of my book.

I wrote back to him, telling him that I had arranged to have a copy of the book sent to him, and I said,

> I have wondered if you have gone back to your Christian studies. Have you found help in reading the teachings of the Lord Jesus? Has your pastor visited you?
>
> I also wonder if you have been able to reflect back to that terrible day in August 1993, to perhaps understand what happened that so terribly affected the lives of so many people. I look forward to hearing from you again.

It was more than a year later, November 2007, before he responded, saying that he had worked hard on trying to examine the "mistakes" he had made and "learn from them."

> When I was 18 I did not think about my actions and their consequences...you could probably label me emotionally retarded...I don't think I was capable of making any "life choices."...None of that excuses me by any means...I hope that you can see that wrong thinking, youth immaturity and personal problems caused me to be cracked by stress...I hope you can understand that I did not

FORGIVENESS—ALWAYS PRESENT TENSE   105

do it because I was pure evil...I am a much better person than I used to be. God works in mysterious ways. I realize that while I am forgiven, I still have to suffer the consequences of my actions...

I was crying as I read this, so great was my sadness that an eighteen-year-old could have caused such pain to himself and others. But then, as I read on, I grew distraught. He asked,

...What do you want to see happen with my life?...In your eyes am I redeemable and worthy of a second chance? I need to know if you would support a commutation of my sentence that would allow me to be parole eligible...

The letter went on a bit longer, but I was incapable of reading any more. I found myself in agony—how could he ask such a thing of me? His request brought me back to that room of cruel death, to the vision of my two loved ones, their bodies destroyed, their lives taken away. He had never said why he killed them. I had forgiven him because he, too, is a child of God. But with this letter, I felt no forgiveness, only bitter anger and pain as I relived the torment of hearing the news that my beloved son and daughter-in-law had been cold-bloodedly murdered. I could hear myself shouting: "If he were out of prison, who's to say he wouldn't buy another gun and kill again?"

Lying flat on the ground, pounding the floor, I screamed at God to help me. There is no way I can describe the journey I began that day, but peace came again when I could accept that there is only one path that would bring me to peace—forgiveness forever. And so I answered,

> Dear Joseph:
>
> I have read and reread your letter of Oct. 3 many times, also sharing it with my four living children. I will comment on it in a minute, but first I want to try to make you understand something of the pain we still suffer. The loss of loved ones, especially by a horrific crime, is a soul-deep, lifelong torment. I don't think you can really comprehend that. We have so many questions about how and why it happened. We deal with the hurt and terrible pain all the time. That never goes away. In fact, I have learned that the pain, for a mother, gets ever worse as I wonder what my kids would look like now, in their fifties, what good work they would have done, whether they would have had a child. I think of how they would still be here on this earth with me if you hadn't invaded their home with your gun and your intent, whatever it was, that left their blood splattered on the wall and in the bed, and their lifeless bodies decaying for a week in that room.
>
> In your letter you have tried to explain where you were at in your 18th year that somehow brought you to kill two good people. It doesn't sound very convincing to me. I think you have to go deeper into your soul to seek the truth of what really happened. These are the questions we would

have—Why did you kill them? You seem to say only that you were a badly mixed up kid with a problem with your father. That I could understand if you had committed a crime of vandalism, or some other not-extreme crime. But murder? No way. I think you have to search deeper in your soul to find the truly honest answer. Were you on drugs? Were you on a power trip that you could sneak into the house that was once your home and steal?

All this being said, I want to reaffirm where we as a family still stand. We are people who cherish life. We never wanted you to face a death penalty. We were willing to forgive you, as a person and a child of God, but never can we forgive the crime. This said, what I hope and pray for is that you continue to grow in your own spiritual life, continuing to do good in the place where you are. We feel that you got the most lenient sentence that anyone who had murdered two people could get, since you are eligible for parole when you are 60. In answer to your question, I have to be honest. There is no way we could support a commutation of your sentence.

I hope you will continue to write to me, and that you will do good work where you are. Stay strong in the love of God. If you write to me again, I shall respond. You are in my prayers.

Four months later, Joseph sent me a brief, but very welcome response. While he never answered my questions, he wrote:

Thank you for taking the time to write to me. You have shown me much kindness. Your letters have helped me. I can only hope that mine have helped you. I had hoped that I could somehow right some of the wrong that I have done. I hope that I have been at least a little successful in this.

Once again I would like to thank you for taking the time to write to me. Your kindness has gone a long way. Thank you and may God bless you.

Shadow

My children and I have made the decision to stay in touch with this young man, now in his thirties, who is so deeply a part of our lives in a way no one of us would ever have chosen. If we have learned anything because of the way he entered our lives, it is that forgiveness is a constant challenge. If ever I were to say I "forgave" someone, I know now that such a statement would have no real meaning. We can only "forgive," because there is no past tense to forgiveness. Because it is such a difficult commandment, it must be constantly and continually renewed. And we must be willing to share what we have learned.

Not long ago I received an e-mail from Sr. Margaret John Kelly of St. John's University, a dear friend. She wrote about a conversation she had had with a university staff accountant. "He told me about an epiphany experience he had a few years ago on this campus which had allowed him to move beyond his persistent anger caused by the tragic murder in the early 1980's of one of his St. John's classmates. As he began to describe the life-changing St. John's event, the place and the speaker, I knew immediately it was your lecture of a few years ago...He summarized his whole epiphany by quoting just one of your sentences.

"Your message was that forgiving is never finished, it must be done every day we live..." Amen!

For what is forgiveness but refusing to build upon the foundation of confusion, misery, and death that we see all around and experience as emanating from the human beings who surround us? What is forgiveness but believing against all evidence, and acting on the belief, that people are really good at heart, even when they show themselves manifestly not to be...

—Joel Marcus

8
HOW FORGIVENESS BRINGS US TO PEACE

This attitude we have been pleading for, this Christian willingness to forgive, has been about the most spiritually redeeming factor in mankind's history . . .

What salvation is there for the world without it? Lacking it, see what history is reduced to! One nation hates another, and the other hates back, and that hate is answered by hate again and that hatred by hatred in return, and so the endless cycle goes on . . . Something transcending hatred, surpassing revenge or even just punishment, must enter in if we are to be saved; and the essence of Christ's saviorhood was this miraculous extra—love even toward enemies, constructive, intelligent good will, determined to break the awful sequence of hatred answered by hatred, and so, to save the world.

—Harry Emerson Fosdick

War has dominated our news and our concerns for so many decades of my life that I have often feared we have never really gotten to know that we call our Lord

Jesus the "Prince of Peace." I especially couldn't help but wonder about that once when I heard a Catholic priest speak about our "right" to defend ourselves in a war with Iraq. When he ended his talk by asking us all to say the famous prayer of St. Francis, "Lord make me an instrument of thy peace..." I felt a curious contradiction, especially since we were the ones who attacked Iraq.

I wonder if he knew that it was a horrendous war—World War I—that brought the Prayer of St. Francis to light. When I heard this priest speak I had just completed work on an expanded version of a book on that war, written by my late son Peter, at the request of the publisher, Facts on File. Immersed in research on this "Great War, the War to End All Wars," I discovered that this prayer for peace had first appeared in 1913 in a small magazine put out in Normandy, France.

It was nearly two years later that *Osservatore Romano*, the official Vatican newspaper, published the prayer. It was picked up the following week by the French daily, *La Croix*, and immediately soared in popularity. As for how the prayer reached the Vatican, that is attributed to the Marquis de la Rochetulon, founder of a Catholic weekly paper, who apparently sent the prayer to Pope Benedict XV, knowing of how he had tried to stop nations from killing millions in that terrible war. The pope had told the warring nations they had created a "horrendous bloodbath which dishonors Europe" and had turned the world into "a hospital and a cemetery." He had tried to make countries see how they were carrying out the "darkest tragedy of human hatred and human madness" with this "useless massacre." He was ignored.

No wonder the Prayer of St. Francis took off, eventually spreading throughout the world! This war that had been raging so furiously and for so long was like no other had ever been. Beginning as a conflict between Serbia and Austria, it had spread to all the major countries of the world, defying all past rules of war and bringing with it unimaginable destruction.

What made this war different was the introduction of something completely new: technology. New "toys" were now available—airplanes, automobiles, wireless, machine guns, killing chemicals—and military use of such inventions changed the very nature of war. It would no longer be limited to soldiers on the battlefield; it would be indiscriminately inclusive, a threat to everyone. Bombardments from the skies would create piles of people dead and wounded. Even more would be killed by starvation as farms and towns were destroyed.

The people, especially in France, where the bulk of the fighting took place, begged for an end to this destruction. Because their leaders had deaf ears, the people had only one to turn to, the Prince of Peace, and so they prayed. The Prayer of St. Francis gave them hope that the horrendous killing would end.

Soldiers, as we know, are the first-line victims of war, obediently following orders that make them kill a person named an "enemy," someone who under other circumstances might be their friend. There was a beautiful moment in World War I, Christmas 1914, when an unofficial cessation of hostilities took place. It began when Catholic and Protestant soldiers in trenches on both sides of the front started singing Christmas songs. They walked into a no-man's land—the strip of land separating them—bringing no weapons, only brandy, chocolates, and musical instruments. For this brief time both sides were joyful, celebrating together the peace brought by the Prince, before they got back to killing each other.

As G. A. Studdert Kennedy, a chaplain who ministered to World War I British soldiers, wrote as the war raged on, "It is trying to keep the hope of Heaven alive in the midst of bloody hell." Hellish circumstances are not particularly conducive to considerations of forgiveness—whether in World War I or in the 130-plus wars the world had endured in the previous century or in the countless wars the world has endured since. In wars, the "enemies" remain faceless; they are certainly not our brethren. And, as we have seen in current wars and armed conflicts, such as those in Africa and in the Middle East, nothing is wrong that destroys an "enemy"; anything is right that wins a war.

Something that becomes very clear in the aftermath of war is how complex forgiveness is. "Forgiveness is a much more serious process than our popular sentimentality makes it out to be," proclaimed the Rev. Harry Emerson Fosdick, preaching at the Riverside Church in New York City at the end of World War II. As he explained, and I paraphrase, we cannot deny that certain conditions must be fulfilled before forgiveness is even possible. Murderers, torturers, those who inflict atrocities on other people, how do we forgive them? Even Jesus was indignant when he saw wrongdoers. Jesus' love for the oppressed and the wronged is clearly evident in the gospel. We have no indication that he doubted the necessity of punishment for unrepentant sinners, though clearly what Jesus ultimately sought was the redemption of evildoers.

Truly, Jesus' life was about teaching us to end injustice, violence, and inequality in this world, to counter hate with forgiveness, compassion, and love, and thus make this a universe of peace.

Our late beloved Pope John Paul II devoted his entire papacy to making known the teaching of Jesus regarding the importance of reconciliation, and never so pointedly as in his January 2002 World Peace Day Message: "To pray for peace is to seek God's forgiveness and to implore the courage to forgive those who have trespassed against us," he wrote, adding, "What sufferings are inflicted on humanity because of the failure to reconcile!"

Many praised him that year, yet many others raised objections: How can forgiveness be possible when someone kills those you love? Isn't it just weakness to forgive? Isn't that letting evildoers get away with their hurting actions?

Nevertheless, the holy father's position was unambiguous: "Forgiveness is above all a personal choice, a decision of the heart to go against the natural instinct to pay back evil with evil... Forgiveness may seem like weakness, but it demands great spiritual strength and moral courage, both in granting it and accepting it."

Throughout the past century many voices have been raised warning about the dire future ahead if we continue our love of war as a way of solving conflict. Famed author H. G. Wells, having been deeply affected by the killings in World War I, wrote of the necessity for "unity in mankind... Sooner or later that unity must come or else plainly men must perish by their own inventions."

Still, he knew what the odds were. In his book he goes on to say: "Set against these motives of unity indeed are other motives entirely antagonistic, the fear and hatred of strange things and peoples, love of and trust in the old traditional thing, patriotisms, race prejudices, suspicions, distrusts—and the elements of spite, scoundrelism, and the utter selfishness that are so strong still in every human soul."

Another voice, this one raised after World War II, was that of writer Lewis Mumford, whose son was killed in that war. The atomic bomb had changed the history of the human race, he believed, and he wrote: "Not to seize power, but to protect and cherish life is the chief aim of man; and the godlike powers that the human race now commands only add to its responsibilities for self discipline and make more imperative a post-magical, post-mechanical, post-nuclear ideology which shall be centered, not on power, but on life."

I could include a hundred more voices crying out to seek an end to "the pagan doctrine and spirit of retaliation," as President Woodrow Wilson—appalled by the punitive Versailles Treaty after World War I—put it. Knowing prophetically that this vindictive treaty, signed by victorious "Christian states," held the seeds for another, more devastating war, he said, partly in anger, partly in sadness, "What it treats with utter ignorance is the Christian doctrine of atonement and redemption."

Jesus spoke continuously of compassion, mercy, forgiveness, and overcoming hate with love. The world talks of vengeance and retaliation. Everything Jesus was about could be said to be in contradiction to the world. Jesus never backed down. He had to show us how to make the world right, and his message was that this will come about only when we, the children of his Father, end conflict, hate, vengeance, and war, and become loving people who seek forgiveness and peace.

Peace Is Central to All Religions

I expanded my reading and found urgings for peace in other religions. Buddhism teaches that true happiness requires us to live in peace with our fellow human beings. Confucianism seeks to ensure the reign of peace throughout the world. Taoism follows suit with the belief that "the good ruler seeks peace and not war, and he rules by persuasion rather than by force." Hinduism maintains that God is a God of peace and desires peace for all people. According to Jainism, "The enlightened will make peace the foundation of their lives. All men should live in peace with their fellows. This is the Lord's desire." Islam offers the same message, that God will guide people to peace "if they will heed him." Then he will "lead them from the darkness of war to the light of peace."

Peace is an important theme in the Hebrew Scriptures. It is mentioned in the books of Psalms, Proverbs, Ecclesiastes, and Isaiah. God commands peace and urges all to work for peace. It is the peaceful life that offers the greatest opportunity for happiness and prosperity. Christians call Jesus the "Prince of Peace." He died to bring us the message that our Father wants us to make this a world without hatred, a world that is not ruled by greed or the egoism that always wants to "even the score," a world of forgiveness. Then we would have a world of peace.

But even as I write this, war is more prevalent than ever. Every day we hear of killings in Iraq, in Afghanistan. The reports are full of hype about how we have to fight, because this is a war against "terror." Putting a name like this on it gives a certain "legitimacy" to the killing and helps to squelch any talk of peace

From the beginning of the Iraq War, we saw very few images of the slaughter of Iraqi soldiers and civilians that took place in that country. One sad story did appear in the *New York Times* on the first Easter Sunday after the start of the war. It carried the chilling headline, "Good Kills," and reported honestly what war means, even in this age of "smart bombs," and "precision weaponry."

Author Peter Maass quoted the Third Battalion's commander, Lt. Col. Byran McCoy, assessing the fighting on that April Sunday, as

> Lordy, heck of a good day. Good kills...We're moving those tanks back a bit to take care of them over there...We're killing them like its going out of style...Sherman said that war is cruelty. There's no sense trying to refine it. The crueler it is, the sooner it's over.

What a chilling reminder this statement is of how stuck we are when the leaders of our nations choose war as a way of settling whatever they perceive to be their "right." As syndicated columnist William Pfaff said, "Even in the self-proclaimed happy, blessed and prosperous United States, fear, hatred and vengeance have, since the attacks of September 2001, become a more powerful combined influence in governing circles than at any time in my life, and it is national policy to do evil for evil."

Then he went on to add, "The promise of both Easter and Passover is mercy—and, fortunately, of unearned mercy. We perhaps do not deserve it, but it is offered." Bless him!

It is time for all of us to focus on the need to choose mercy over vengeance, and Catholics should be leaders in this call for mercy, which begins with forgiveness. Since April 30, 2000, we have celebrated Divine Mercy Sunday one week after Easter. Pope John Paul II instituted this feast after having canonized Sr. Faustina, the Polish nun who kept a diary of her encounters with Jesus, who told her "You are the secretary of my mercy," and then went on to speak to her virtually non-stop of God's mercy and forgiveness.

During the next years of her short life—she died at age thirty-three—Sr. Faustina kept a diary in which she wrote down what Jesus told her. His message was certainly in contradiction to the world's message, and it was a message for all: "I demand from you deeds of mercy which are to arise out of love for Me. You are to show mercy to your neighbors always and everywhere. You must not shrink from this or try to excuse or absolve yourself from it."

Are we listening? Jesus is telling us that we can't keep opting for revenge in the name of human justice, nor can we gain security by hating those we consider to be our enemies. He wants us to grasp that mercy is needed, for it has everything to do with rising toward God, letting hatred go so that we never sink to a level of distortion that generates more hatred. This is a tough call, given that our instinct is always to want to "even the score."

Yet, if we desire to be one with God, we must be merciful. So long as we believe ourselves to be "at war," it is all too easy to justify killing "the enemy," trashing a country, taking over its resources, and to do all this while using

God's name to bless us—even as we remain self-righteously mired in hatred, the state of soul that so grieves our God.

"By placing unattended rage before God we place both our unjust enemy and our own vengeful self face to face with a God who loves and does justice," writes theologian Miroslav Volf. "Hidden in the dark chambers of our hearts and nourished by a system of darkness, hate grows and seeks to infest everything with its hellish will to exclusion.

"In the light of the justice and love of God, however," he adds, "hate recedes and the seed is planted for the miracle of forgiveness."

Who "Deserves" Forgiveness?

Because I have become known for my work against the death penalty, I have been often challenged by someone telling me, usually in anger, that there are certain people who do not deserve forgiveness. A good man, a divorced father whose children blame him for the breakup of their parents' marriage and refuse to forgive him, asked me, "How does one get over or through the conviction that 'This person doesn't deserve forgiveness for what he or she did'?"

He went on to explain:

> Of course, what the person "did" might have been a single action or something that was repeated over a long period of time. I have no idea how one can convince another to get past this mindset—except I feel it's a bit of idolatry. We believe God forgives and our God is a God of forgiveness. That a

human—no matter how harmed or damaged—
would say, "This person, this action, doesn't deserve forgiveness" is to assume God's role.

Sister Helen Prejean writes of death row inmates who have the worst moment of their life
freeze-framed by single incident. Of course the
"incident," being murder, is no ordinary "incident." Still, my point is that individuals routinely
convict others to the death row of unforgiveness, a
life sentence with no possibility of parole.
Individuals set up their own court, in their own
mind, weigh the testimony, and render the sentence: *I condemn you to life without the possibility of
forgiveness.*

Whack the imaginary gavel and that's it. This
court-of-the-mind has no higher court, no court of
appeal. None is needed. The decision has been ren-
dered and it's assumed that God will certainly
agree.

I could feel the pain coming through his words, and I
wondered—who had less peace, this man or his unforgiving children? At least he had an understanding of how
wrong condemnation by a refusal to forgive is, especially in
families.

His words reminded me of a scene from the theater production of *Camelot*. King Arthur has been betrayed by his
wife Guinevere, who has fallen in love with Lancelot. In this
scene Arthur is alone on the stage, the depth of his anger and
his rage evident as he rants about the disloyalty and infidelity
of his wife and his friend. Then, suddenly, he stops. The ex-

pression on his face, a look of sheer anger, softens, and after a moment of silence he asks, "But what of *their* pain?"

Then King Arthur shows he is truly a king, for he puts love and mercy ahead of vengeance, forgiving his wife and his friend, not allowing them to be vengefully killed for their betrayal, but instead imposing the rightful punishment of banishment from his kingdom.

Many people have been victims of great injustice, and it is hard to criticize someone who has been in that kind of situation. Still, when you meet a person who has endured the suffering of injustice and yet is forgiving, the experience is unforgettable. I had such an experience a few years ago when I met Rubin "Hurricane" Carter briefly at a Christopher Award evening in New York. This man had spent twenty years in solitary confinement on death row for a murder he had not committed. When he was found innocent and released, he wrote his story, which was then made into a movie starring Denzel Washington as Hurricane Carter.

"Until I saw Denzel up on the screen, I didn't know how good looking I was," he was quoted as saying with a smile. When he was asked if he had forgiven all the people who had contributed to his wrongful conviction, his response was unequivocal: "I don't accuse them of having done anything to me. They weren't judging me for something I did; they were judging me in there for the color of my skin. Period...I have nothing against anybody, there's no reason. I'm alive, I'm healthy, and I'm happy."

This fine man then went on to explain that "bitterness will consume its own vessel...Once you're in the state of anger, you can be angry at anything. You can't sleep, you can't walk, you can't talk, and you can't forgive." Hurricane Carter chose to forgive and find peace.

So often when I read of the horrors of wars, past and present, I wonder how people who have been or are victims of war's atrocities can forgive the ones in charge who choose war as a way of gaining the power they want.

Newspaper headlines read like daily obituary pages, tallying how many people were killed the previous day in all the hate-filled, war-torn places of our world. I get on my knees as I finish reading, remembering the atrocities of the many wars that have taken place during my lifetime, none worse than World War II.

I would guess few people know the story of Nazi military men gone mad during that war when they took over the town of Nowogrodek in Poland. To assert their power and, no doubt, to put their hatred for the church into action, they marched a community of nuns who had long worked in the town, eleven Sisters of the Holy Family of Nazareth, out to a wooded field and shot them point-blank, dumping their bodies into a common grave.

I had never even heard of the eleven martyrs of Nowogrodek until recently. I had even missed seeing a small item in the paper back in the year 2000 that had mentioned them among the saintly people Pope John Paul II would be beatifying for their bravery, motivated by love of others. I first learned about these "Blessed Martyrs" from Sr. M. Agnese, the provincial superior of the Sisters of the Holy Family of Nazareth based in Monroe, Connecticut. Sr. Agnese had called to invite me to speak at a community day of recollection, the theme of which was to be reconciliation and forgiveness.

When I arrived at the convent, Sr. Agnese told me about the community's foundress, Mother Frances Siedliska, a woman from Poland who had died at age sixty in 1902. She had wanted to found a community of sisters that would serve the human family, from children to the old, always serving as witnesses of God's love as revealed in the holy family of Nazareth.

Then Sr. Agnese told me about the sisters of Nowogrodek. Though this was a Polish town characterized by ethnic and religious diversity, the sisters, who had arrived in 1929, had always had wonderful relationships with the people. It was the war that brought evil and destruction to this place.

The Nazi terror began with the extermination of the Jews in the town. Then, knowing that Polish and Soviet partisans were a threat to them, the Germans executed sixty people, including two Catholic priests, on July 31, 1942. This was followed by intensified Nazi oppression, resulting within a year in a new wave of 120 arrests, mostly of fathers and sons torn from their families. The people came to the sisters and it is known that Sr. Stella, the community superior, literally prayed, "Oh God, if sacrifice of life is needed, accept it from us who are free from family obligations and spare those who have wives and children in their care. We are praying for this."

Unexpectedly, the Germans appeared at the convent, rounded up the sisters, escorted them to Gestapo headquarters, and confined them there for the night. At daybreak on August 1, 1943, the sisters were driven to nearby woods and shot, execution-style. The community affirms, "God accepted the sacrifice offered on behalf of their brethren..." Unbelievably, "all those for whom they sacrificed their lives were saved!"

War is hell, indeed, but "meeting" these eleven Blessed Martyrs was assurance once again for me that God lets Heaven break through in unexplainable ways. In fact, if we examine the history of World War II we can discover many people who confronted the godless crimes of the Nazis with amazing near-mystical goodness, people like Etty Hillesum.

Born into a family of Dutch Jews, Etty could have escaped the fate of the Jewish people in Amsterdam at the hands of the Nazis, but she chose to stay and help her neighbors by working in a local hospital. Eventually, the Nazis arrested and imprisoned her and her family, finally putting them on a "transport" to Auschwitz. It is reported that, during that last journey, Etty threw a postcard out the train window. On the postcard she had written, "We left the camp singing."

Etty kept a notebook in the prison camp, and her diaries have been preserved. I can't help but wonder what gives a young woman the courage and wisdom to write words like these: "Ultimately, we have just one moral duty: to reclaim large areas of peace in ourselves, more and more peace, and to reflect it towards others. And the more peace there is in us, the more peace there will also be in our troubled world... We should be willing to act as a balm for all wounds."

Etty Hillesum died in Auschwitz at the age of twenty-nine.

Fr. Alfred Delp, a Jesuit priest, who became a member of a resistance group in Nazi Germany, was also imprisoned in a Gestapo prison and kept there for a long period of time, even after his trial and sentence of death. According to biographer Alan C. Mitchell, "a philosopher obsessed with the place of humans in history, and who believed that humans created their own history, was now a victim of a history he was desperately trying to change. A man of God, whose whole life was given in service to others, was now at the mercy of a godless regime."

Fr. Delp was killed by the Nazis in 1945. He was thirty-eight years old. Many of his writings have been preserved, as has this one, where he speaks of all humankind, who must turn to "the healing forgiveness of God":

> God bids us place our hope of mercy in the mercy we are prepared to show. The sins of the world must vanish with transcendental guilt so that the world now and then may breathe again. As far as we are concerned this means that we must refrain from all bitterness against those who have wronged us. I bear them no grudge; I forgive even that charlatan who made such a travesty of German justice. They even arouse my pity. But I pity still more the people who have delivered themselves and their holy spirit into the hands of such monsters. God help us.

In his last hours, Fr. Delp wrote to his family and friends, asking forgiveness of all for the times he may have "failed them," or been "arrogant...or proud and overbearing..." But he spoke also of his "offense"—"...that I refused to accept that accumulation of arrogance, pride and force that is the Nazi way of life, and that I did this as a Christian and a Jesuit...Germany will be reborn, once this time has passed, in a new form based on reality with Christ and his Church recognized again as being the answer to the secret yearning of this earth and its people..."

Fr. Alfred Delp went to his death on February 2, 1945 after having celebrated a noontime Mass, again with the prayer of forgiveness on his lips and the peace of the Lord in his heart.

His prediction that Germany would be "reborn" has come to pass, but what he really prayed for—the end of war—has not. Today, we are immersed in the horror of knowing that daily deaths from our technologically advanced weapons keep mounting in conflicts around the world, and in a war in Iraq, a war begun by our own nation. The grim milestone reported in newspapers on Easter Sunday 2008 was that, only a few days after the fifth anniversary of our invasion of Iraq, the death toll of our soldiers had exceeded four thousand. The hundreds of thousands of Iraqi civilians killed in this war goes mainly unreported in our country.

We must ask God's forgiveness for starting and fighting wars, even as we struggle to ask forgiveness for those who then retaliate against their "enemy" with cruelty.

The call to follow Christ always means a call to share the work of forgiving men their sins. Forgiveness is the Christlike suffering which it is the Christian's duty to bear.
                                        —*Dietrich Bonhoeffer*

9
FORGIVENESS—
THE KEY
TO GOD'S KINGDOM

I suspect that the forgiveness Jesus asks of us begins with our seeing the ones who have harmed us ... as fully human ... We may still be hurt, afraid and angry. The feelings may linger for a lifetime. No matter how hurt, afraid or angry we are, no human being is ever a monster. We may find it difficult to love, but through the eyes of faith we can begin to see that every man and woman is always and everywhere loved as much by God as are our greatest saints. That love alone is worthy of our greatest efforts to understand and to forgive.

—Matt Malone, SJ, whose brother Joe was killed by a drunk driver

In August 1993 when I got the terrible news that my son and his wife had been murdered, my faith was challenged more radically than it ever had been before. Now I found myself in a totally new place, facing a raw, real confrontation within my soul. Could I ever forgive the killer?

If I lived by my faith, I would have to say with Jesus, "Father, forgive him, for he didn't know what he was doing." I would have to believe, as Jesus said, that evil is overcome by good. But, in total honesty—now that the issue of forgiveness would never again be academic, removed, or simple—could I say from my heart, "Father, forgive the murderer"?

This was the gut-wrenching question I grappled with in my prison of anger, pain, desolate sadness, and beautiful memories, not just of John and Nancy, but of my deceased son Peter, too. All the uncertainty regarding where I was and how I would ever find an answer put me in a bleak place. Yet, remembering the joy my sons had been to me kept me saying "thanks" to the One who had given them life and shared this gift of their lives with me.

At Mass one Sunday, I prayed in thanksgiving to God for the "temporary gift" of my deceased children. At that very moment I felt a sudden jolt, like a slap in the face, and I heard the words, "It was a permanent gift." I had been corrected, a priest told me later, and so, through my tears, I could say, "Thanks be to God." In recognizing this "permanent gift" I was given the grace to know that I could forgive. I had the power not to let an assassin erode who I am or put a wedge between me and my God.

I came to understand that true forgiveness means countering the horror of evil—whatever that evil may be—with love, as Jesus taught. Learning this took time. It was like being on a journey, the most difficult journey I had ever undertaken, because I was constantly fighting overwhelming feelings, sometimes of hatred and sometimes of dread, for all that had happened. Yet, I came to really understand why forgiveness was essential. I knew that if I didn't forgive, permanently, I would cease to be the human being I was created to be. I would jeopardize my destiny, to one day be in God's heavenly kingdom. I came to trust that, with God's help, I had what I needed to help me never let hate or revenge destroy my capacity to become the person God wants me to be. And I saw that the paradox of forgiveness is that we cannot be healed if we do not forgive others, but that if we do forgive, it is we, ourselves, who benefit the most.

I found much wisdom about forgiveness in many places, one being some writings from a movement called "A Course on Miracles," founded in 1965 precisely to heal suffering at its source through the "spiritual practice of forgiveness in our relationships."

According to this program,

> Forgiveness is the bridge of healing that carries us from fear to love, pain to joy, loneliness and isolation to connectedness and communion, conflict and turmoil to peace. Forgiveness is a choice we make to look at a brother, or a situation, or ourselves, through the eyes of love instead of through eyes of judgment—to share the perception of the Holy Spirit rather than that of the ego.

I am in complete agreement with these words and would add only one more thing: we must pray for an inner strength to help sustain us, since we often falter in our resolve to forgive.

Murder at the Columbine School

In April 1999 people throughout our country were shocked and horrified at breaking news of the killing that had taken place at a high school in Columbine, Colorado. As reporters began to get more information on what had happened, we knew we were seeing the worst school shooting in U.S. history. Two high school students, Dylan Klebold and Eric Harris, had gone on a deliberate killing spree, pumping bullets into whoever was in their path. Before they were "stopped dead" themselves, the school had become a morgue—with twelve students and one teacher killed.

The first to be killed was seventeen-year-old Rachel Scott, a beautiful young girl who, as it turned out, had kept a diary in which her writings had proclaimed, somewhat prophetically, her belief that her life "would have an impact on the world."

As I was completing research for my own book, I had the good fortune of meeting Rachel Scott's uncle, Larry Scott, whose life changed completely after his niece was murdered. A former construction worker, he left that profession behind so that he could dedicate himself to bringing what he calls "Rachel's Challenge" to students in over one hundred colleges, high schools, and junior high schools each year.

Six weeks before Rachel was killed, she had written down what she titled "My Ethics, My Code of Life," her uncle said. Part of what she wrote was: "Look for the best in others ... Eliminate prejudice ... Start a chain reaction of kindness and compassion ... We can't change others but we can influence them ... Dare to dream for your life ..."

Surprisingly, even as a child, she had written, "Someday, I will touch millions of people's hearts."

Larry Scott told of how Rachel had chosen Ann Frank as a role model and was influenced by the words of this teenager, killed by the Nazis during World War II. Ann Frank had said, "Always give something, even if it is only kindness." Those words really influenced Rachel, for she wrote, "I'm going to have an impact...People will never know how far a little kindness can go...I have this theory that if one person can go out of their way to show compassion, then it will start a chain reaction of the same." Rachel's definition of compassion, her uncle said, included two words, "forgiving and loving."

Then Mr. Scott told an amazing story. Shortly after the Columbine killings, a businessman from Ohio called Rachel's family out of the blue to tell them of a dream he had had about Rachel. He had seen her quite clearly in the dream. From her eyes tears flowed to the ground, but coming up from the ground was new growth—"life was coming as new growth from her tears," he said, in astonishment.

The dream itself was striking. But there's more. Seven days later, the sheriff's department returned Rachel's backpack to her family. In it they found Rachel's diary. On the last page was a picture she had drawn, and the image was exactly as the man from Ohio had described it: thirteen clear tears, and a rose—new life—coming up from the ground! Had I not experienced in my own life so many of the miraculous ways in which the Lord works to give us "signs" of his love, I would perhaps have had my doubts about all this.

Now Larry Scott and Rachel's brother Craig, a young film-maker, have brought Rachel's story to millions, mainly to school students. "We challenge the kids to forgive each other and other people," Mr. Scott told me. "If you don't forgive, you walk in bitterness all your life. With forgiveness, you have no cancer eating at your insides. We can make the choice to get better, or get bitter."

Expressing a strong faith, Larry Scott went on: "We all have to grab on to something more powerful than ourselves. In our situation, that's God. Sometimes stories come into the world for a reason, and we have to find that reason. Let's help the world with this."

The family of Rachel Scott is, indeed, doing much to show the world the relationship between forgiveness and God's kingdom, thanks to their beloved, martyred, teenaged relative who left them this message in her own amazing way.

When God Seems Like a "Cosmic Sadist"

I had never heard God referred to as a "cosmic sadist" until I read *A Grief Observed*, a book written by C. S. Lewis, the Irish-born Oxford University teacher/scholar—known even to children for his "Chronicles of Narnia." Lewis's despairing definition of God was formed in his tortured heart after his wife Joy died in 1960.

Thanks to film director Richard Attenborough's movie *Shadowlands*, many people had the opportunity to learn about the happiness that came late into the life of C. S. Lewis when he met and married Joy Gresham. The film, which received two Academy Award nominations, is a very moving love story that deals with the inescapable truth that happiness and pain are intertwined.

I had been introduced to the writings of C. S. Lewis by my high school music teacher, Sr. Jerome Joseph, many decades ago. One day in school I met her walking down the hallway. She had a big smile on her face. When I asked her why, she told me she was reading a very funny book called *The Screwtape Letters*. Knowing how much I loved reading, she said she'd pass the book on to me as soon as she finished it.

Well, she did, and then it was I who was walking down the hallway smiling. This was my introduction to C. S. Lewis, and I became an immediate fan as I read about Screwtape, a seasoned devil, trying to train a neophyte devil, Wormwood, in the ways of deviltry!

But the book that really touched me was Lewis's auto-biographical *Surprised by Joy*. This book tells of his lonely early youth, his mother's death when he was only nine, and his distant father, with whom he and his only sibling, a brother, could never really have a positive or nurturing relationship.

His pain and sense of total loss at seeing his mother dead put him in a wasteland when it came to faith, and this book tells of the ensuing spiritual journey that led him to atheism and then back to Christianity. Always he was searching for "joy," a term that was not to be confused with pleasure or happiness.

For C. S. Lewis, joy had one overriding characteristic, "that any one who has experienced it will want it again." He writes of a time and place when he had "tasted" joy, and he calls this "the fullest possession we can know on earth." In his later writings, he summarizes his search for joy in one profound sentence: "Joy is the serious business of heaven."

The fact that the woman who came late into his life was named "Joy" was a "coincidence" that could not have been lost on C. S. Lewis, who equated joy with heaven. Nothing happens by accident. By the time he had reached his early fifties, this man, so famed for his spiritual insights, particularly regarding suffering—he was a World War I veteran!—had managed to keep himself protected for decades from the pain he had experienced after his mother's death.

But I think Lewis would say that God saw to it that he would continue to mature and grow spiritually. God sent Joy to him, and they were married in April 1956.

Then, after four brief, intensely happy years, Joy died of cancer. Lewis went into a rage against God. As a way of coping with the agony of loss he was experiencing, he turned to the one thing he could do—he put all his feelings into writing. In the depths of his despair, he kept a deeply honest journal, which he titled *A Grief Observed*, and in which he chronicled his pain, his uncertainties, and even, I believe, his doubts about the God he had believed in. He was struggling to forgive God!

He writes, "You never know how much you really believe anything until its truth or falsehood becomes a matter of life and death to you." Then he asks, "Why is He so present a commander in our time of prosperity and so very absent a help in time of trouble?" Finally, despairing, he wonders, "Perhaps the bereaved ought to be isolated in special settlements like lepers... Time after time when he seemed most gracious, He was really preparing the next torture... the Cosmic Sadist."

As his anger mounts he continues his rant, saying that all he wants is "the happy past restored." Revealing his tattered faith, he pleads, "Don't come talking to me about the consolations of religion or I shall suspect that you don't understand."

As he comes closer to "forgiving" God, Lewis reflects that "You can't see anything properly while your eyes are blurred with tears." Then comes his great acceptance of how extraordinary pain, what he calls "passionate grief," does not "link us with the dead *but cuts us off from them*... God has not been trying an experiment on my faith or love in order to find out their quality. He knew it already. It was I who didn't," he confesses, and then, ultimately, he arrives at peace.

It is not at all surprising to me that C. S. Lewis would have rediscovered his faith, for so much of his life had been immersed in his understanding of the Christian faith. He had much earlier addressed the reality of intense spiritual pain in his 1943 book, *Mere Christianity*, in which he wrote that we shouldn't be surprised if we're in for "a rough ride." I had learned about this from my late son Peter, who had left me these words from C. S. Lewis, along with his suicide tape:

When a man turns to Christ and seems to be getting on pretty well...he often feels that it would now be natural if things went fairly smoothly. When troubles come along—illnesses, money troubles, new kinds of temptation—he is disappointed...why now?...Because God is forcing him on, or up, to a higher level; putting him into situations where he will have to be very much braver, or more patient, or more loving, than he ever dreamed of being before. It seems to us all unnecessary; but that is because we have not yet had the slightest notion of the tremendous thing he means to make of us.

In one of the most memorable passages C. S. Lewis ever wrote, he uses a parable, saying that we are a "living house" that God has come into to rebuild. At first every remodeling he takes on makes sense.

> But presently he starts knocking the house about in a way that hurts abominably and does not seem to make sense. What on earth is he up to?
>
> The explanation is that he is building quite a different house from the one you thought of . . . You thought you were going to be made into a decent little cottage; but he is building a palace. He intends to come and live in it himself.

Peter signed the pages he left for me with these words of C. S. Lewis, simply, "Pete."

My guess is that C. S. Lewis would have gladly chosen the "little cottage," if his beloved Joy could have been there alive with him. But God was making him into a "palace," with one requirement. He had to "forgive" God for having left him on this earth without Joy.

Long before meeting Joy he had confronted forgiveness, saying,

> I am telling you what Christianity is. I did not invent it. And there, right in the middle of it, I find, "Forgive us our sins as we forgive those that sin against us." There is no slightest suggestion that we are offered forgiveness on any other terms. It is made perfectly clear that if we do not forgive, we shall not be forgiven. There are no two ways about it.

And so C. S. Lewis learned the hardest truth of all, as I did, that sometimes the one we have to forgive is the One who gave us all we ever wanted, and then took it back to himself, forcing us to restart the journey to his kingdom with newly blank roadmaps.

C. S. Lewis died on the same day as President John Kennedy, November 22, 1963.

Seeking Forgiveness, Being Rejected

There is a scene in the film about the master composer Beethoven, *Immortal Beloved*, in which he is in a carriage going to meet with the love of his life. Unfortunately, the carriage gets bogged down and encounters all sorts of delays. He finally arrives at the building and races up the rear stairs—at the exact moment she is coming down the front stairs. The movie shows that they never did get together. They were unable to forgive one another—each thinking the other didn't care.

Things like this don't happen only in movies. A friend related how, in a time before cell phones, her uncle had an appointment to meet his best friend at lunchtime at a certain spot. "My uncle went to the appointed place and waited his whole lunch hour, but his friend never showed. Not only that, he never apologized," she said.

"There was so much anger between them that it took these best friends a full year before they got in touch to talk about this. What they found out was that they'd both gone to the meeting place during their lunch hour. It's just that my uncle's lunch began at noon, and his friend's began at one o'clock." My friend commented, "I think stubbornness is a real impediment to forgiveness or reconciliation."

Miscommunications, misunderstandings—how often these lead to permanent hostility, all too often between family members. Sometimes one will try to "fix" the damage, even acknowledging personal responsibility in the conflict, seeking forgiveness. Sadly, many times, the response is a resounding rejection.

In my work on forgiveness over nearly two decades, I have come to understand how very complex the subject is. One man I highly respect asked me, "When a person is seeking forgiveness from someone who is not available to give it, what is the person to do?" He explained why he was asking this question, and it had to do with his very young life:

A year or so after I was born, my mother had a troubled pregnancy from which she never regained her health. She struggled for the rest of her life before dying when I was four. Although I may not have been conscious of a sense of abandonment while living through the experience, I learned in a therapist's office that my mother's death was in fact a form of abandonment, depriving me of an important part of the nurturing to which I was entitled.

Still, the strongest emotion I can come up with for myself is disappointment and regret. I did attend one session of an abandonment therapy group and heard the pain and outrage of those who had been abandoned by a parent. They focused on their anger—forgiveness never came up at all—and anger like this is something I have never before or since seen.

My friend continued: "When we think of forgiveness, we think of going to a person and saying, 'I'm sorry.' And that person responds in some way. But," he went on to say, "as I asked before, when a person needs to forgive someone who is not available to receive the forgiveness, what is the person to do?" Then, answering for himself, he said: "The person seeking to forgive one who will never be there to receive it has to get over it and get on with their life."

Not exactly. This really falls into the category of excusing oneself from the hard work of forgiveness. "Christian commitment permits no such rationalism," writes New Testament author Christopher D. Marshall. He explains what he means by "such rationalism" and why it is incompatible with Christianity:

> Only God can forgive, [one might] reason; it is beyond the capacity of ordinary mortals to rise above their pain and bitterness to confer forgiveness on their abusers. But...the entire Christian message centers on forgiveness, which it views as both gift and demand. God's *offer* of forgiveness to sinners, and God's *demand* that those who receive this gift practice forgiveness in their relationships with others, are inseparably connected.
>
> Jesus articulates this forgiveness equation most succinctly: "Forgive, and you will be forgiven." But he cautions, "If you do not forgive others, neither will your Father forgive your trespasses." It is because of this interdependence between God's gift of salvation and the activity of forgiveness, and also because of the sheer struggle involved to make it

work in practice, that one can fairly say that forgiveness is "the demand of the Gospel that pinches
the hardest."

At a very young age I had an experience that visually
demonstrated this truth to me. I grew up in the city of
Albany, New York, and when I was a child my father would
often drive me to Altamont, where there was a shrine we
called simply La Salette. It commemorated an appearance
of the Blessed Virgin Mary to two young farm children on
September 19, 1846, in the obscure village of La Salette in
the Alps of southeast France. The children saw a circle of
light and a beautiful woman sitting on a stone. She was crying, and she had her face buried in her hands. When she
looked up, she told the children not to be afraid. She said
they should tell the people that if they continued to offend
her Son, they would have hunger and pain. But if they did
good things, they would have great blessings.

Mary was wearing a crucifix around her neck, and the
children gave a striking description of this. Jesus was on the
cross, to the left of the cross there was a pair of pincers, and
to the right, a hammer. The children were told that the
hammer represented our sins, which had nailed Jesus to the
cross. But the pincers—*an instrument for pulling out nails, an
instrument that would cause pain when these nails were pulled
out*—represented our sorrow, repentance, and forgiveness.

I was too young when my father took me to the shrine
to understand this, but life went on to teach me that forgiveness is the demand of the gospel that "pinches the
hardest!" Still, it remains a non-negotiable command from
the Lord himself.

Courageous Journeys to Forgiveness

It is not hard to understand why someone who has been severely injured in body, mind, or spirit would choose to harden his or her heart and want to reject the very idea of forgiveness. In the words of Adolfo Quezada,

> When we forgive, we do not excuse; we do not condone; we do not sanction. First the hurt, the hate, the wanting to retaliate, all of these feelings must have their day in court. Forgiveness must come from a heart that is open and willing to confront the truth. We cannot dull our senses and lose touch with our feelings and call this forgiveness...Forgiveness is not a declaration of trust...
>
> In fact, those whom we are forgiving don't even have to know about our forgiveness to be forgiven...Our forgiveness still frees us to move ahead. Forgiveness changes the heart of the forgiver even if it does not change the forgiven.

I have found that what is most difficult for almost all people to understand is how anyone who has been a "victim" of any kind of abuse or serious pain would even want to forgive the one who scarred them. Forgiveness is, indeed, "radical," as Adolfo Quezada states, as he goes on to explain its importance: "We have it in our power to let the spirit of forgiveness take over the world or we can block it right where we stand. We are the gateway through which the mercy of God flows into the lives of others."

Scripture scholar Christopher D. Marshall has also emphasized the importance of the response of victims if forgiveness, as Jesus taught it, is to ever be accepted as his crucial commandment. In his classic work, *Beyond Retribution: A New Testament Vision for Justice, Crime and Punishment*, Christopher Marshall writes:

> Forgiveness is what happens when the victim of some hurtful action freely chooses to release the perpetrator of that action from the bondage of guilt, gives up his or her own feelings of ill will, and surrenders any attempt to hurt or damage the perpetrator in return...Forgiveness is a "gift for" someone else, the guilty party, a gift of release from the burden of guilt and its destructive consequences in the offender's own life. The power of forgiveness comes from its gratuitous nature. It is freely given, an act of generosity. It is not deserved...It comes as a free offering on the part of the victim.

I personally have been amazed at how many stories of forgiveness I have found merely by looking for them with an open mind. Several years ago I gave a talk on the death penalty to a group called Delaware Citizens Opposed to the Death Penalty, and since then I have read many stories of forgiveness in the newsletter put out by the group. One such story was written by Kim Brook, a prison volunteer, who, like myself, is the mother of a murdered child. On March 25, 1995, Kim's sixteen-year-old daughter Nicole was stabbed to death by a sixteen-year-old boy named LeVaughn.

"My only child lay dying on the floor of the living room, her eyes still open. The last sight she saw that day was the face of the young man who was killing her. This young man, whom I had never met in my life, came into my life that day and changed my life forever," said this mother, who was told a week later that the district attorney was seeking the death penalty for the killer.

Kim Brook was tormented, for, as she explains, "I don't believe in murder. Murder is murder no matter how you look at it. It was no more right for me to take LeVaughn's life than it was for him to take Nicole's life. I did not need revenge."

She was present at the trial of this angry young man, and she was there when he was found guilty of second-degree murder and sentenced to thirty-eight years in prison, with no probation. Then this mother stood at the podium to address the court and the judge, and I have no doubt that they were probably shocked, as she began reading what she had written. As she later explained, "God spoke to my heart."

I told LeVaughn that I was not angry with him, but that I felt very hurt. I told him that I had compassion for him and that I hoped that he could somehow find a way to turn his life around. And lastly I told him that I would be praying for him.

The face that had been so full of anger was now looking at me in disbelief, and the anger was gone. When I walked away from the courthouse that day, I knew that God had given both of us a gift. It was the gift of forgiveness. I was able to forgive the

young man who murdered my daughter. Not because he asked me to, but because it was what God
wanted for both of us. God was never going to be
able to use me if I was angry.

"Forgiveness brings peace. And with that peace comes
overwhelming joy, the joy of knowing that God will forgive
me just as I have forgiven," concluded this mother, speaking clearly from her heart.

Several years ago, reading the *New York Times*, I came
across the photo of a man with one eye sealed shut. The
caption read, "Chris Carrier, who survived a shooting and
stabbing in 1974."

The story accompanying the photo began by saying
that Chris Carrier had recently gone to a nursing home in
North Miami Beach to visit his friend, David McAllister, a
blind, frail, and lonely seventy-seven-year-old man. Chris
took along some of the man's favorite food, comforted him,
and made sure he was being well taken care of. That was
the last time he saw his friend, who died later that night.

The story that followed was chilling. It turned out
that, only recently, Mr. McAllister had confessed to a
crime he had committed twenty-two years earlier, that of
abducting, stabbing, and shooting Chris Carrier, then a
ten-year old boy, in the head, and leaving him in the
Everglades. The boy had been blinded in the left eye as a
result of the shooting.

The crime had taken place on the last Friday before
Christmas vacation. Chris had then been a fifth-grade student at Westminster Christian School. He had gotten off

the school bus and was walking home when Mr. McAllister picked him up, stabbed him with an ice pick, drove him to a desolate spot, then shot the boy in the head from behind before leaving him for dead. Chris, who was unconscious for six days, miraculously survived and was found by a farmer who happened to be driving by.

Ironically, David McAllister had been considered a prime suspect in the disappearance of the boy by Major Charles Scherer of the Coral Gables police, the original detective on the case. Mr. McAllister had a long criminal record, and had also been dismissed by Chris Carrier's father, who had hired him to take care of an elderly uncle, making retaliation a motive. But there was no physical evidence linking Mr. McAllister to the crime.

Years later, when Major Scherer heard that Mr. McAllister was a patient in the nursing home, he went there to talk to him, and the old man confessed, expressing sorrow for what he had done. When Chris Carrier heard of this, he decided to visit the man who had left him for dead. He carried with him no ill will, only forgiveness. "It wasn't hard for me to show compassion. I told him that from now on there would be nothing like anger or revenge between us, nothing but a new friendship," said this man, married and the father of two daughters, who had also worked as a youth minister.

Chris Carrier acknowledged that he had "shocked people" by forgiving and then befriending the man who had almost killed him. Chris visited his "new friend" frequently in the few weeks he had left to live. "I tried to let him know he had a friend," he said.

Forgiving One's Self

Not to be forgotten in all this is the sorrow and pain endured by someone who has committed a terrible crime and is now repentant, seeking forgiveness. The most difficult step in the process is the very first—forgiving oneself. Vonda White, a long time friend whom I have never met in person, has been imprisoned for nearly thirty years in a California prison. I bonded with her because, like me, she was a single parent of six children. Imprisoned for a crime she had committed, she nevertheless turned to God to help her live a good life, even though she was behind bars. Through friends, I learned she had been a consistently model prisoner who had spent her many years in prison doing good work and helping others. Vonda wrote and said:

> Forgiveness is a critical issue for an offender such as I am. It may seem to be a contradiction, but it is difficult to forgive others when one is weighed down with the burden of forgiving one's self and having a difficult time of it. Still, it is many times easier to forgive others and to make one's amends when one feels forgiven as well.
>
> The truth is, forgiveness, in matters both small and great, brings the greatest joy and satisfaction. Forgiveness proceeds from grace and an open heart that wants the best for all. Yet, I sometimes think we hold on to unforgiveness in the mistaken belief that to forgive is unfair. We don't like to see others, or even ourselves, "get away with" wrong actions.

I believe that I began to truly heal from the effects of my own guilty responsibility when I came to know that God still loved me and had forgiven me. And HOW did I know this? I knew it when I began to understand and see how God was blessing me in my earnest endeavors—and how could I not forgive myself and extend that forgiveness to others when I was being so richly graced?

Forgiveness stories like these and so many others that I have heard in the course of my lifetime have been for me, I can truly say, clear signs that Jesus' rule of forgiveness is the essential one that links us to our Father in heaven.

The forgiveness of God which Jesus proclaims and which he urges humankind to imitate does not focus on sin but is a direct appeal to human goodness. To understand forgiveness in the context of human goodness it is necessary to explore the central symbol of Jesus' personality and mission—the Kingdom of God... The Kingdom is not a thing to be observed but the experience of God with human activity... The experience of forgiveness which Jesus proclaims is a possibility for humankind not because we are a sinful people but because we are good people who sin.

—Fr. John Shea

POSTSCRIPT

*Retributive justice seeks to check and punish evil; the justice
commended in the New Testament is empowered with
self-giving, long-suffering, redemptive love that seeks to
overcome evil with good, to repair the damage done by sin,
and to restore peace to human relationships.*
                                    —Christopher D. Marshall

A s I write these final words, I have been reading of the
horrors, and again seeing some of the photos, of the
gruesome abuse that went on at the Abu Ghraib prison
after the United States declared war in Iraq, all docu-
mented in a new book, *Standard Operating Procedure*, by
Philip Gourevitch and Errol Morris.

In a *New York Times* review of the book, Michiko
Kakutani wrote:

> Within days of 9/11, Vice President Dick Cheney
> declared that the administration intended to work
> "the dark side," and in the ensuing months, Mr.
> Gourevitch writes, "the vice-president's legal coun-

sel, David Addington, presided over the production
of a series of memorandums, which argued against
several centuries of American executive practice and
constitutional jurisprudence by asserting that the
president enjoyed essentially absolute power in
wartime, including the authority to sanction torture.

This is chilling reading for a Christian—or anyone, for
that matter—seeing in print justification of behavior that
treats people in a way that is so contrary to everything that
Jesus taught. I am convinced that our only hope for a world
that will not continue to destroy goodness is to take seriously and live by Christ's amazing words in the Sermon on
the Mount, words that continually emphasize forgiveness.
As Erik Kolbell, a psychotherapist and former minister of
social justice at Riverside Church in Manhattan, writes,
Jesus on the Mount delivered

> what would become one of the most important ser-
> mons the world has ever known...
>   If you want to see what the kingdom of God
> could look like, if you want to live a blessed life, he
> told them, take the world as you know it and turn
> it on its head. That is to say, imagine it free of the
> tyranny, poverty, loneliness, and greed that now
> hold it in thrall. Imagine it loosed of the unholy
> trinity of ignorance, arrogance, and indifference
> that conspire to suffocate all remnants of hope.
> Imagine the hungry fed and the just vindicated, the
> poor satisfied, and the pure sanctified. Imagine a
> world governed by an urge for compassion rather

than a will to power. Imagine all this, he tells them, *because this is what God imagines,* because these are the people God has deemed blessed and this is what God wants us to make of ourselves. Imagine such a world, he told them, and then, having imagined it, live in accordance with it. Live it into being. Live as though the world is turned upside down, because when you do you will see the kingdom, if not come, then at least coming.

The author summarizes the message of the Sermon on the Mount by saying that "Christ paints a picture where, with God's blessing, common people do their best to redeem an imperfect world,"—ending war, greed, terror, torture, killing…

Still, people are quick to ask: Why should we forgive instead of condemning these horrors? German theologian Hans Küng provides an answer—after asking a related question:

Why does grace come before law? Because God himself does not condemn, but forgives…The parables of Jesus were more than mere symbols of the timeless idea of a loving Father-God. These parables expressed in words what occurred in Jesus' actions, in his acceptance of sinners: forgiveness.

The forgiving and liberating love of God for sinners became an event in Jesus' words and deeds. Not punishment for the wicked, but justification of sinners; here already is the dawning of God's kingdom, the approach of God's justice…Man ought— so to speak—to copy God's giving and forgiving in his own giving and forgiving.

I can say that Hans Küng personally opened my mind to consider new possibilities about the God who made us, for I once had the privilege of being one of his "pupils" for five days. This was back in the summer of 1966, when Fr. Küng, along with two Protestant theologians, the Revs. Harvey Cox and Martin Marty, were the guest discussion leaders at a Contemporary Theology Institute at Loyola College in Montreal.

One thing Jesus did, Fr. Küng stated, was to "boldly announce God's forgiveness ... to assure the individual sinner directly of forgiveness." It is no wonder, Fr. Küng pointed out, that Jesus was accused of arrogance and blasphemy, that his opponents, the "defenders of law, right and morality" would say, "Who does this man think he is?" Jesus was certainly not surprised that they would immediately get to work on how they could "liquidate him."

Jesus' uncompromising words on how forgiveness opens the door to his Father's world has been and will remain his most difficult and challenging teaching. For most of us, not a day goes by when forgiveness, in one of its countless forms, doesn't crop up, though most of us, thankfully, don't have to grapple with it in the context of serious hurt. It is at those times, however, that we come face to face with ourselves, learning and seeing who we are as clearly as if we were looking into a mirror.

Much has been written about forgiveness and help is there for all who want it. In an important new book, titled *Surprised by Hope*, my former teacher N. T. Wright again emphasizes forgiveness, saying:

> ... Forgiveness is not a moral rule that comes with sanctions attached. God doesn't deal with us on the

basis of abstract codes and rules like that. Forgiveness is a way of life, God's way *to* life; and if you close your heart to forgiveness, why, then you close your heart to forgiveness! That is the point of the terrifying parable in Matthew 18, about the slave who had been forgiven millions but then dragged a colleague into court to settle a debt of a few pence. If you lock up the piano because you don't want to play to somebody else, how can God play to you?

That is why we pray, *"Forgive us our trespasses, as we forgive those who trespass against us."* That isn't a bargain we make with God. It's a fact of human life. Not to forgive is to shut down a faculty in the innermost person, which happens to be the same faculty that can receive God's forgiveness.

Throughout my life I have read countless books to gain some insight and perhaps wisdom that might help me in the dark times when my prayer was only "Lord, I believe, help my unbelief." One day, in a time after the tragic deaths of my children, when I was struggling to hold onto Jesus and his words, I picked up a book entitled *The Outline of History*, written by H. G. Wells in 1920. I had read that H. G. Wells was not a religious believer, but toward the end of this book, in a section on the beginnings of Christianity, he had this to say about Jesus:

He was like some terrible moral huntsman, digging mankind out of the snug burrows in which they had lived hitherto. In the white blaze of this kingdom of his there was to be no property, no privilege, no pride and precedence; no motive indeed, and no reward but love. Is it any wonder that men were dazzled and blinded and cried out against him? Even his disciples cried out when he would not spare them the light. Is it any wonder that the priests realized that between this man and themselves there was no choice but that he or priestcraft should perish? Is it any wonder that the Roman soldiers, confronted and amazed by something soaring over their comprehension and threatening all their disciplines, should take refuge in wild laughter, and crown him with thorns and robe him in purple and make a mock Caesar of him?

For to take him seriously was to enter upon a strange and alarming life, to abandon habits, to control instincts and impulses, to essay an incredible happiness...

Is it any wonder that to this day, this Galilean is too much for our small hearts?

To accept Jesus, Wells went on to say, meant that one would have to make the "most revolutionary changes in his way of living."

Those words hit me so strongly, as it suddenly became clear to me that there was a way out of my dark days, but only if I took on "revolutionary changes," focusing not on my losses, my pain, but on the work ahead that could be done if I did it Jesus' way. To this day, in my prayers, I include a "thank you" to H. G. Wells.

Another book I picked up at around the same time was published some eighty years ago by E. Stanley Jones, an evangelical missionary, after he had been asked by a publisher to write a book answering this question: "In the light of scientific research, can our gospel stand up under this search for fact?"

He immediately answered that yes, that the gospel "is founded on fact, the Fact of Christ...The Christian word is Life because our gospel is founded on life and it imparts life...a new spirit born at Pentecost."

Then he went on to explain that "Pentecost means power—power to forgive injuries, to keep an unsoured spirit amid the deepest injustices, to overcome evil with good, hate by love, and the world by a cross."

Reading this wise man's words, I again realized that when Jesus said we must forgive "seventy times seven," this was not a suggestion. The challenge that faces us daily as Christians is to think about what Jesus meant by forgiveness, and to pray for the courage to act on it again and again—seventy times seven!

[Jesus] taught men and his words had the ring of reality about them. Others quoted authorities; he taught with the authority of his own insight. Others came seeking truth; he came proclaiming it...He lived with them, and before them, and in his words they heard the Word—the Word that he was. When he spoke of love they knew what it meant, for they had seen it—had seen it in his face, in his deeds, in him. When he spoke of God, they felt his presence, for he came not proclaiming God; he brought him...

—E. Stanley Jones

NOTES

INTRODUCTION

xi   G. K. Chesterton, *Orthodoxy* (San Francisco: Ignatius Press, 1995) 101–2.

1. JESUS' MISSION—TO REVEAL HIS FATHER

1   T. R. Glover, *The Jesus of History* (New York: Grosset & Dunlap, 1917) 113.

2   Henri-Daniel Rops, *Jesus and His Times* (New York: E. P. Dutton, 1954) 321.

3   G. K. Chesterton, *The Everlasting Man* (Garden City, NY: Image Books, by special arrangement with Dodd, Mead and Co., 1955) 210.

6   Glover, *The Jesus of History*, 113.

7   C. S. Lewis, *A Grief Observed* (New York: Bantam, 1980) 67.

13   N. T. Wright, *Jesus and the Victory of God* (Minneapolis, MN: Fortress, 1996) 127.

14   Ibid., 272.

15   Ibid., 127.

15   Norman Goodall, *One Man's Testimony* (New York: Harper Bros., 1949) 123.

15   Erik Kolbell, *What Jesus Meant* (Louisville, KY: Westminster John Knox Press, 2003) 22–23.

2. THE CRUCIAL FACE-OFF—EVIL VS. FORGIVENESS

18   John Hick, *Evil and the God of Love* (New York: Harper & Row, 1966).

21   Hans Küng, *On Being a Christian* (Garden City, NY: Doubleday and Co., 1976) 230–31.

21–22   Alvin Plantinga, "God, Evil, and the Metaphysics of Freedom," in *The Problem of Evil*, ed. Marilyn McCord Adams and Robert Merrihew Adams (New York: Oxford University Press, 1990) 85.

24   Hans Küng, *On Being a Christian*, 434–35.

25   Albert Nolan, *Jesus Before Christianity* (Maryknoll, NY: Orbis Books, 2001) 10.

25   Simone Weil, *Gravity and Grace*, trans. Emma Crawford (New York: Routledge, 2002) 76.

26   Ibid., 27.

26   Diogenes Allen, "Natural Evil and the Love of God," in Adams and Adams, *The Problem of Evil*, 201.

27   Joel Marcus, *Jesus and the Holocaust* (New York: Doubleday, 1997) 74.

3. HUMAN WAYS VS. JESUS' WAY OF DEALING WITH HURT AND INJUSTICE

28   Terrence J. Rynne, *Gandhi and Jesus: The Saving Power of Nonviolence* (Maryknoll, NY: Orbis Books, 2008) 157.

29   Eugenia Price, *No Pat Answers* (Grand Rapids, MI: Zondervan, 1972).

29   Andre Dubus, *Broken Vessels* (Boston: David R. Godine, Inc., 1992) 138.

29–30   Edmund Burke, "A Letter to a Noble Lord," *Works of the Right Hon. Edmund Burke* (London: S. Holdsworth, 1837) 2:268.

34   Walter Wink, *Engaging the Powers* (Minneapolis, MN: Fortress, 1992) 199.

36–37   Ibid., 266–67.

38   James Douglass, *The Nonviolent Coming of God* (Maryknoll, NY: Orbis Books, 1991).

42   Dietrich Bonhoeffer, *Letters and Papers from Prison* (New York: Macmillan, 1953).

4. WHEN THE HEART BLOCKS FORGIVENESS

44–45   David P. Barash, *Natural Selections: Selfish Altruists, Honest Liars, and Other Realities of Evolution* (New York: Bellevue Literary Press, 2007).

45–46   Robert Barron, *The Strangest Way: Walking the Christian Path* (Maryknoll, NY: Orbis Books, 2002) 97.

47–48   Fr. Rick Potts, Editorial, *Liguorian* magazine (April 2008).

51   Frederick Buechner, *The Sacred Journey* (New York: Harper Collins, 1991) 2, 3.

56   Barron, *The Strangest Way*, 84–85.

57   Henri J. M. Nouwen, *Can You Drink the Cup?* (Notre Dame, IN: Ave Maria Press, 1996) 104, 50.

58   Ibid., 74–75.

5. HOW FORGIVENESS FREES THE HEART, MIND, BODY, AND SOUL

61   Harry Emerson Fosdick, *The Man from Nazareth* (New York: Harper & Bros., 1949).

69   Gertrude Huntington, *News-Times*, Danbury, CT (October 5, 2006).

71–72   Immaculée Ilibagiza, *Left to Tell* (Carlsbad, CA: Hay House Publishers, 2007) 95, 94, 111.

74   Johann Christoph Arnold, *Seventy Times Seven: The Power of Forgiveness* (Farmington, PA: Plough Publishing House, 1997) 111–12.

6. GOD'S NON-NEGOTIABLE RULE FOR HUMAN INTERACTION

78   Rig Veda 5.85.7–8.

78-79   *The Way of Life, According to Laotzu*, translated by Witter Bynner (New York: Penguin Putnam, 1944) 60.

79   *Sayings of Buddha* (Mt. Vernon, NY: Peter Pauper Press, 1957).

79–80   *The Thoughts of the Emperor M. Aurelius Antoninus*, trans. George Long (London: Ticknor and Fields, 1864) 44, 69.

80   Ibid., 68.

81   Ibid., 25.

88   Earl Conrad, *The Invention of the Negro* (New York: Paul S. Eriksson, Inc., 1966).

90   William James, *The Varieties of Religious Experience* (New York: Collier Books, 1961) 277.

90   E. Stanley Jones, *The Christ of Every Road* (New York: Abingdon, 1930).

7. FORGIVENESS—ALWAYS PRESENT TENSE

91   Robert Barron, *The Strangest Way: Walking the Christian Path* (Maryknoll, NY: Orbis Books, 2002) 96.

96   John Lingard, "Execution of Mary, Queen of Scots," in *The Sixth Reader*, ed. George Stillman Hillard (Boston: Brewer and Tileston, 1873) 280–81.

99   Jason Song, "Her Holocaust Pardon Inspires Others," *Los Angeles Times* (January 6, 2008).

100   Sigmund Spaeth, *Stories Behind the World's Great Music* (Whitefish, MT: Kessinger Publishing, 2005) 68.

109   Joel Marcus, *Jesus and the Holocaust* (New York: Doubleday, 1997).

8. HOW FORGIVENESS BRINGS US TO PEACE

110   Harry Emerson Fosdick, *On Being Fit to Live With* (New York: Harper & Bros., 1946).

114–15 H. G. Wells, *Outline of History* (New York: Macmillan, 1921) 1087–88.

115   Lewis Mumford, "How War Began," in *Adventures of the Mind*, ed. Richard Thruelsen and John Kobler (New York: Alfred A. Knopf, 1960).

116   S. E. Frost, Jr., ed., *The Sacred Writings of the World's Great Religions* (New York: McGraw Hill, 1972).

117   Peter Maass, "Good Kills," *New York Times Magazine* (April 20, 2003).

117–18 William Pfaff, *Fear, Anger and Failure: A Chronicle in the Bush Administration's War Against Terror from the Atacks in September 2001 to Defeat in Baghdad* (New York: Algora Pub., 2004).

119   Miroslav Volf, *Exclusion and Embrace: A Theological Exploration of Identity, Otherness and Reconciliation*, (Nashville: Abingdon Press, 1996) 124.

124   Etty Hillesum, *An Interrupted Life* (New York: Holt, 1996) 226.

125   Alan C. Mitchell, "Preface," in *Alfred Delp, SJ: Prison Writings* (Maryknoll, NY: Orbis Books, 2004) xvii.

125–26   *Alfred Delp, SJ: Prison Writings* (Maryknoll, NY: Orbis Books, 2004) 112, 161–62.

126   Dietrich Bonhoeffer, *The Cost of Discipleship* (New York: MacMillan, 1963) 100.

9. FORGIVENESS—THE KEY TO GOD'S KINGDOM

127   Matt Malone, SJ, "The Father of Mercies: A Lenten Reflection on Forgiveness," *America Magazine* (March 7, 2005).

129   "A Course on Miracles," Foundations for Inner Peace, Inc., 1975.

134–35   C. S. Lewis, *A Grief Observed* (New York: Bantam Books, 1980).

135–36   C. S. Lewis, *Mere Christianity* (New York: Macmillan, 1952).

139–40   Christopher D. Marshall, *Beyond Retribution: A New Testament Vision for Justice, Crime and Punishment* (Grand Rapids, MI: Wm. B. Eerdmans Publishing, 2001) 263.

141   Adolfo Quezada, *Heart Peace: Embracing Life's Adversities* (Totowa, NJ: Resurrection Press, 1999).

142   Marshall, *Beyond Retribution*, 264-65.

147   Fr. John Shea, *The Challenge of Jesus* (Chicago: Thomas More Press, 1984).

POSTSCRIPT

148   Christopher D. Marshall, *Beyond Retribution: A New Testament Vision for Justice, Crime and Punishment* (Grand Rapids, MI: Wm. B. Eerdmans Publishing, 2001) 259.

148–49   Michiko Kakutani, review of *Standard Operating Procedure*, by Philip Gourevitch and Errol Morris, *New York Times* (May 14, 2008).

149–50   Erik Kolbell, *What Jesus Meant* (Louisville, KY: Westminster John Knox Press, 2003) 21.

150   Hans Küng, *On Being a Christian* (Garden City, NY: Doubleday and Co., 1976) 276.

151–52   N. T. Wright, *Surprised by Hope* (New York: Harper One, 2008) 288.

152–53   H. G. Wells, *The Outline of History* (New York: Macmillan, 1921) 505.

154   E. Stanley Jones, *The Christ of Every Road* (New York: Abingdon, 1930).